Milly Francis

The Life & Times of the Creek Pocahontas

Dale Cox

Edited by Savannah Brininstool

2013

ISBN-13: 978-0615894058
ISBN-10: 0615894054

Visit the author online at:

www.exploresouthernhistory.com

Old Kitchen Books
4523 Oak Grove Road
Bascom, Florida 32423

Blessed are the merciful: for they shall obtain mercy.
Matthew 5:7

*This book is respectfully dedicated to
the members of the Wakulla County Historical Society,
the staff of San Marcos de Apalache Historic State Park
and the faculty and students of Bacone College.*

Table of Contents

Introduction

The story of Milly Francis is a story of America. Her memory is claimed by four states and three nations. Thousands of young women born between 1818 and 1860 bore her name. Her father was a prophet who met the royalty of England and Russia before meeting his fate at the end of Andrew Jackson's rope. Her mother could not speak English, but was forced to turn to the people who had executed her husband for food to feed her starving family. Milly's husband gave his life in the service of a country that drove his family west on the Trail of Tears. She had eight children, but only three lived to become adults.

With her own eyes, Milly saw such noted figures of the early 19th century as Tecumseh, William Weatherford, Edward Nicolls, Robert Ambrister, Andrew Jackson and Osceola. David Moniac, the first American Indian to graduate from the U.S. Military Academy at West Point, was her cousin. The great Creek Indian leader Alexander McGillivray was her great-uncle.

And yet none of these individuals would ever exhibit the one thing that Milly Francis gave to Americans of her generation, a show of mercy so profound that it caused an entire country to begin a long, painful reconsideration of its attitudes about its original inhabitants. In the spring of 1818, when she saved the life of a young American soldier named Duncan McCrimmon, Milly caused newspaper editors across the nation to ponder how such human qualities could exist in the heart of a "savage."

Thirty years later Milly Francis became the first woman ever to receive a special medal of honor from the United States Congress. It was an honor that would not be repeated until the Civil War.

The story of Milly Francis, however, is more than the tale of a brave and selfless act carried out by a young woman to save the life of a young man. It is the story of the great upheaval that took place in the Creek Nation in 1813-1814, of the First Seminole War and of the brutal cruelty inflicted on the Creek people during the Trail of Tears. It is a heartbreaking yet inspirational tale of the survival of one woman in a time of horror and of how she lost so much, but never gave up her dignity and hope. It is a story that should inspire us all.

I first began researching the story of Milly Francis many years ago. The idea for this book grew as, in my own journeys in life, I found myself repeatedly crossing paths with her. When I walked the site of Holy Ground, I crossed her footsteps. She had lived there when she was only nine years old. A strange fog clung low to the ground that day, as if the Prophet's magic from 200 years ago was still brewing. A chill passed over me at the thought.

From the places of her childhood along the Alabama River to the scene of her death on the Arkansas River in Oklahoma, I have walked Milly's path. Pensacola, Fort Gadsden, San Marcos de Apalache, Tallassee, the Hickory Ground, Memphis, Little Rock, the Ozarks and the Ouachita Mountains of Arkansas, Fort Smith, Fort Gibson, the prairies of Oklahoma and finally the hill tops of the city of Muskogee were all part of her journey. As I visited each of these places during my own journey in life, I came to realize just how remarkable she was and how far she traveled.

It is my hope that this book will open a door to her life for a new generation. Her memory is fading from our hearts, but Milly Francis is a person worthy of remembrance. She was pure, honest and merciful in a time of great evil and cynicism. I believe that after reading her story, you will come to agree.

Many people assisted in the research, writing and editing phases of this book, my sincere thanks are extended to all. Savannah Brininstool served as primary editor and, as she did in our collaboration earlier this year on *The Scott Massacre of 1817*, has done a phenomenal job. My mother, Pearl Cox, was kind enough to read the first draft of the manuscript. My sons, William and Alan Cox, accompanied me on many of my journeys into the past and I am grateful to them both.

Appreciation must be extended to the staff members of the following institutions: Florida State Archives, Georgia State Archives, Alabama State Archives, John C. Pace Library of the University of West Florida, Florida History Library at the University of Florida, Georgia Historical Society in Savannah, Bradley Library in Columbus (GA), Willard Library in Evansville (IN), Fort Smith Public Library in Fort Smith (AR), Oklahoma Historical Society (OK), Muskogee Nation of Oklahoma, Richland Library in Columbia (SC), Fort Smith National Historic Site (AR), Gulf Islands National Seashore (FL), San Marcos de

Apalache Historic State Park (FL), Fort Gadsden Historic Site (FL), Fort Gibson State Historic Site (OK), the Library of Congress and the National Archives

Thank you also to my friends and readers for your encouragement and support through often difficult times. You will never know how much you mean to me..

May God bless and keep you.

Dale Cox
September 15, 2013

Milly Francis

The Life & Times of the Creek Pocahontas

Chapter One

Daughter of the Prophet

THIS IS THE STORY OF A REMARKABLE EVENT that took place on the banks of Florida's Wakulla River in March 1818 and of its lasting impact on American life and culture. A young Creek Indian woman named Milly Francis, daughter of the Alabama Prophet Josiah Francis, saved the life of an American soldier. This demonstration of mercy forced white Americans to begin a long reconsideration and evolution of their thoughts and attitudes regarding North America's original inhabitants. The kindness shown to a stranger by Milly Francis drew widespread acclaim and inspired the amazement of the media of the day. It also ignited a national debate when Andrew Jackson and the U.S. Army responded by hanging her father at Fort St. Marks the following month. This debate would rage for decades and in some ways still echoes today. In the last days of her life, Milly Francis became the first American woman ever to receive a medal of honor from the United States Congress.

Milly Francis was born in Alabama in around 1803. Her father, Josiah Francis, was an artisan who worked with metals. Her mother, Polly Moniac, was the half-sister of the noted trader and ferry operator Samuel Moniac. Milly's first

1

cousin, David Moniac, later became the first American Indian to graduate from the U.S. Military Academy at West Point. She also was related through her mother's family to the famed Creek leaders Alexander McGillivray and William Weatherford.

Both her mother and father were mestizos, a racial classification that means they were of both European and American Indian descent. In their day they were called "half breeds" and writers of the 19th and early 20th centuries often pointed out that "white blood" flowed in Milly's veins. It was their way of trying to explain how the daughter of a man regarded in his lifetime as a savage fanatic could demonstrate such a gentle quality as mercy. In short, it was white America's way of humanizing a young woman who – by the standards of the day – was regarded as something considerably less than human.

The Francis family lived in the Alabama towns of the Creek Nation. Located along the banks of the Alabama River just below its head at the confluence of the Coosa and Tallapoosa Rivers, these towns were part of the loosely organized Creek Confederacy, but were independent from the Muskogee or Upper Creeks in language, customs and manners. When first encountered by the Spanish explorer Hernando de Soto in 1541, the Alabama (or Alibamo) were living near the Choctaw and Chickasaw in present-day Mississippi. They battled the European intruders and de Soto's capture of the Alabama stockade was given prominence in the chronicles of his expedition. By 1675, when Spanish missionaries penetrated the region west of the Apalachicola and Chattahoochee Rivers, the Alabama and related Coushatta (Koasati, Coosada) had migrated east to the river that still bears their name. The reason for this migration is unclear, but likely was due to conflict with the powerful Choctaw and Chickasaw.

By the time Josiah Francis was a young warrior, some of the Alabama and Coushatta had already migrated west of the Mississippi River to Texas, where their descendants still live today. Like many of the mestizos then living in the Creek Nation, he was raised and in turn he raised his own family with influences from both Indian and white culture. Francis, for example, could speak multiple languages including Alabama, Muskogee, English and Spanish. The latter two were necessary for him to be able to communicate with government officials and representatives of the trading firm of Panton, Leslie & Company, as well as with his own father. The former were needed to communicate with the people of his own town and with the Upper Creeks at large. Milly Francis, by the time she was fifteen, was fluent in all of these languages, undoubtedly due to the influence of her father, since her mother could speak neither English nor Spanish.

The Creek Nation was at the height of its power during the decade in which Milly Francis was born. Alexander McGillivray had forged a stronger central government for the confederacy and had carried out such successful military operations against the whites that President George Washington was forced to negotiate with the Creeks as equals. The result was the Treaty of New York, a remarkable document that recognized the Creek Nation as an independent entity of the same category as England, France or Spain. It established territorial limits along the lines demanded by McGillivray and assured two decades of peace between the Creeks and the United States. A little known secret amendment to the treaty also authorized a permanent salary for McGillivray and provided educational funds for select young men from his nation. Among them was David Francis, the father of Josiah.

The treaty also called for the introduction among the Creeks of what the whites called the "plan of civilization." Directed by Washington's newly appointed Agent for Indian Affairs, Colonel Benjamin Hawkins of North Carolina, the plan was designed to build a European-style culture among the Indians. The plow, spinning wheel and loom were introduced to the Creeks, along with white crops and lifestyles. By the time Milly Francis was born in around 1803, the "plan" had proved quite successful, particularly among the Lower Creeks who lived along the Chattahoochee and Flint Rivers.

Many of the mestizos living in the territory of the Upper Creeks also adopted Hawkins' recommendations. William Weatherford, Zachariah McGirth, Samuel Moniac, David Tait, Peter McQueen and Josiah Francis all became wealthy men by the standards of their day and location. They owned swine, horses and herds of cattle. They lived in comfortable cabins and homes that in many cases were of better design and construction than those of the white frontiersmen who lived around the fringes of the Nation. Their style of dress was little different than that of famous "long hunters" like Daniel Boone and David Crockett. The British Museum preserves several articles of clothing that once belonged to Josiah Francis, including a long hunting shirt of deer skin, moccasins, leggings and a belt. Crockett, Boone or any of the other frontiersmen of their day would have been comfortable wearing the same.

The mestizo women lived much as did white women on the frontier. They cooked and cleaned and tended the garden and fields. They usually wore simple dresses of homespun cotton, with soft moccasins on their feet and jewelry of gold, silver, copper and other metals. Since Josiah Francis was noted for his artistry and ability to work with metal, the jewelry collections of the women of his family likely benefitted from his skills.

The fields and gardens of the Alabama towns were regarded by Benjamin Hawkins as being the best in the Nation. The production of cotton was expanding among them by the decade of Milly's birth and they also grew corn, pumpkins, peas, squash, beans and tobacco. Many of the larger farms produced in such abundance that a successful trade was carried on with merchants in the Spanish cities of Pensacola and Mobile as well as with the white and mestizo traders – like Josiah Francis and Samuel Moniac – who operated stores in the Nation stocked with supplies from Panton, Leslie & Company – later John Forbes & Company – the large English trading firm based in Pensacola. These traders also purchased deerskins in large numbers, along with other pelts, and sold merchandise for gold and silver.

The decade from 1800 to 1810 was one of growing prosperity and peace in the Creek Nation. Relations with the whites were generally good and, aside from occasional raids or minor confrontations with the neighboring Choctaws and Cherokees, the Creeks were at peace with adjacent American Indian nations. In the first year of the next decade, however, everything changed.

Milly Francis was still a young girl in 1811 when she witnessed a series of the most remarkable events in American history. They began in the summer of that year, not long after the annual Busk or Green Corn Festival. A long tradition among the Creeks, this festival celebrated the ripening of the corn harvest and the lighting of the fire for a new year. It was the time when the men took the black drink and when every fire in each town was extinguished and then relighted from a new flame. At around the time of the Busk in 1811, however, a strange phenomenon appeared in the sky.

As observers in both America and Europe watched, the famed Comet of 1811 grew night after night as it rocketed through space on its elliptical journey around the sun. The Creeks, of course, had seen comets, but this one was unlike any they had seen before. Reports of the time indicate it was the most brilliant that anyone then living had ever seen and paintings from 1811 even show it glowing in the sky over Europe. Legend holds that famed Shawnee leader Tecumseh predicted the coming of the comet in his visit to the Creeks, angrily warning their leaders that they would soon see his arm of fire in the sky. It would be a sign to them that they should have listened to his admonitions and joined in his war against the whites.

Sometimes legends are just legends. The comet was visible to the Creeks before Tecumseh arrived to speak at their annual council that fall. The Shawnee leader may have pointed to the celestial object during his speeches to the Creek Council, but he would not have predicted its appearance since it already could be seen. The coming of Tecumseh, however, was the second major event that took place among the Creeks during the eighth year of Milly Francis's life and he appeared immediately on the heels of the arrival of the comet.[1]

Much has been written about Tecumseh's visit to the Creeks. Confusion over the year he appeared and the language he used in his speeches to their council persists to this day. Although he grew in status over the coming years, Tecumseh was still under the shadow of his brother when he came South in 1811. Tenskwatawa, the powerful Shawnee Prophet, was the brother of Tecumseh and it was at his behest that Tecumseh left Vincennes, Indiana, in June 1811 and went south to visit the Chickasaw, Choctaw and Creek Indians.

Originally called Lalawithika ("Noisy Rattle"), the man who would become the Shawnee Prophet was an overweight town drunk who had lost an eye in an accident with an arrow. Viewed with disdain by his family and neighbors, he was so lost in a world of alcohol that all who knew him expected that he would die soon from his excesses. In 1808, however, something dramatic happened to Lalawithika, something so profound that it changed the course of American history.[2]

After a day of severe liquor consumption, Lalawithika fell into an alcohol-induced coma and died. Family members could detect no pulse or sign of breath and word spread that he had finally succumbed to death from the alcohol that had destroyed his life. Preparations were made for a funeral and family members were preparing his body for burial. Suddenly, to the shock off all, Lalawithika came back from the dead.

As family and friends listened in amazement, he told a remarkable story of having died and gone to the next world. There he met the Master of Life and was shown a paradise filled with game and honey where those who lived good lives went after they died. He also was shown a hell where drunks and other evil doers were tortured for eternity. Molten lead being poured down the throats of alcoholics and other sinners received similar punishments.

Lalawithika came back with a message from the Master of Life for all American Indians. He changed his name to Tenskwatawa ("Open Door") and began to preach, first to his own family and village and then to others. He told of his spiritual journey and announced that he had given up liquor and everything else associated with whites. He would eat only natural foods and drink only water. The Master of Life had told him that the Indians should return to their native ways and give up the things and ways of the whites. If they did so, and if they united, they would be able to preserve their lives and lands and save their eternal souls.

This was the message that Tecumseh brought to the Creeks in 1811. Although many writers later claimed that he urged war with the whites to drive them into the sea, in truth he delivered a message of peace and called for the Creeks to forge an alliance with other nations and to return to their traditional ways:

...Tecumseh, in the square of Tuckaubatchee, delivered their talk. They told the Creeks not to do any injury to the Americans; to be in peace and friendship with them; not even to steal a bell from any one of any color. Let the white men on this continent manage their affairs their own way. Let the red people manage their affairs their own way....[3]

This account of Tecumseh's final speech to the council was provided to Benjamin Hawkins by chiefs who were present. Despite later claims by Sam Dale and others, no white man was present when the Shawnee leader spoke. Claims that he urged war are counter to everything known about every speech given by Tecumseh or the Prophet himself in 1811 and the preceding years. The version given by Hawkins, however, is very consistent with written accounts of the speeches they gave elsewhere. They urged peace, a return to native ways, and unity. They also urged a total break from the whites and the refusal to sell another inch of Indian land without the agreement of all of the nations.

It is unlikely that Milly actually heard Tecumseh speak at Tuckabatchee, but she undoubtedly saw him there. He was one of a remarkable series of figures from the pages of American history who also touched the pages of her life's story.

The Creek leaders admitted to Hawkins that they didn't understand much of Tecumseh's speech. He talked of visitations with the Master of Life, they reported, and did not make sense. They concluded he was crazy and wished him well as he started his journey home to the Shawnee country of Indiana, Illinois and Ohio.

Contrary to much of what was written in subsequent years, Tecumseh's great speech to the Creeks had no real immediate impact. A few warriors and chiefs were curious, but for the most part life in the Nation went on as normal. Some writers have tried to give the Shawnee more influence in coming events in the Creek Nation by moving the date of his visit to 1812 or suggesting that he returned to the Creek council that year. Tecumseh's visit to the Creeks was in 1811 and he never returned. By the time he reached his home in Indiana from that visit, the Battle of Tippecanoe had been fought and the Prophet's town destroyed.

The timing of Tecumseh's visit in 1811 also casts doubt on claims by many both in the 19th century and today that he brought secret messages from the British designed to bring the Creeks into a war with the United States. The War of 1812 had not begun in 1811 when he visited the Creeks and the British were so tied up dealing with Napoleon in Europe that they had no interest in a war with the Americans. It was the U.S. that declared war the following year, not Great Britain. The latter nation had no emissaries among the Shawnee in 1811 to urge war against the United States.

While Tecumseh's visit did not shake the Creeks, a series of events that soon followed definitely spread alarm in the Nation. The great New Madrid earthquakes of 1811-1812 were the largest ever felt in North America. When the ground moved and shook in December 1811, an entire section of the Mississippi River flowed backwards. Trees were turned upside down so that their roots stuck in the air and their branches were buried in mud. In New York, the shaking made the church bells ring and in Washington, D.C., Congressmen ran out of the Capitol believing that they were somehow under attack. Chimneys fell in Charleston, Savannah and New Orleans.[4]

The earthquakes could be felt in the Creek Nation and Milly Francis felt them on repeated occasions. As the Creeks discussed the shaking of the ground with each other and sought an explanation for them, some began to wonder if the Shawnee Prophet really had visited with the Master of Life. Seekaboo, a lesser prophet who remained behind to minister to the Creeks when Tecumseh departed, encouraged such thoughts. Delegations from the upper towns began to make their way north to hear the Prophet in person. They left curious but returned as converts.

Among those quietly harboring such thoughts about the meaning of the great events of 1811-1812 was Josiah Francis. The Alabama towns were on the route that Creeks and Shawnees took on their visits to each other. This allowed the Alabama towns to receive news from the Midwest faster than the other Creek towns. Francis visited with Seekaboo and may even have gone to see the Prophet himself. The exact chain of events is murky and mysterious. Those turning to the new religion kept their actions secret from the traditional leaders of the Nation and especially from the whites. This secrecy increased as news arrived from the Shawnee towns that the United States and Great Britain had gone to war. If the tribes could unite, then with British support they could end the westward expansion of the American nation once and for all.

Milly's father was a man who had lived his life in two cultures, white and Creek. He had known Alexander McGillivray and remembered how the great leader had gone to war against the United States when white settlers refused to recognize Creek borders and land claims. He remembered how McGillivray had united the Nation under his leadership and how his warriors devastated the American frontiers so severely that George Washington was forced to negotiate.

As he looked around, Francis saw reason for great concern. The Big Warrior, Little Prince and other traditional leaders of the Creek Nation had accepted the "plan of civilization" espoused by Benjamin Hawkins, a plan that ran directly counter to the teachings of the Shawnee Prophet. Francis himself had benefited from that plan, but as he considered the current situation, he realized that the mighty Creek Nation was being destroyed. The Federal Road had been opened through the heart of Creek territory and white settlers were pouring through the Nation to open new settlements on its western border. Pressure was mounting from Georgia for more land. The Tennessee settlements were spreading south. And with them the whites brought their poisons. Rum was more plentiful in the Creek Nation than ever before and once proud chiefs and warriors were succumbing to its influences.

Francis considered these things and as he did so, the teachings of the Shawnee Prophet grew in his mind as a way – the only way – to reverse the trend that would eventually swamp and destroy the Creek Nation. Whether from Seekaboo or during a visit to see the Prophet in person, Francis learned the tenants of the new religion. He spoke with the Master of Life himself and waded into the rivers and creeks to hear the voices of the water spirits. In the fall of 1812, Josiah Francis set fire to his home and barns, slaughtered his livestock and announced to his fellow Alabamas that he had become a prophet.

Milly Francis was around nine years old when her father had his conversion and it must have been a fascinating yet terrifying time for her. Her home and everything she had ever known was destroyed and her family returned to the traditional ways of the Creeks. Pork and beef disappeared from their table and instead they ate venison, squirrel and bear. Her cotton dresses were replaced with garments of deer skin. The spinning wheels and looms were thrown into the fire. Milly's life changed overnight from one comparable to those of white girls living on the fringes of her nation to one more in line with the lives of her ancestors.

Josiah Francis came to be called Hillis Hadjo ("Warrior of Crazy Medicine") by other Creeks. He withdrew from his hereditary town near the head of the Alabama River to a new location on the south side of the river about halfway between the modern cities of Montgomery and Selma. There he planted a new settlement, one consistent with his teachings, and named it Ecanachaca ("Holy Ground"). His converts followed and the settlement slowly began to grow. Word spread in the nation that the Prophet Francis and his followers had begun to dance the "Dance of the Indians of the Lakes."

---

[1] The visibility of the comet was noted in the *Alexandria Herald*, July 4, 1811, p. 4.

[2] Summarized from R. David Edmunds, *The Shawnee Prophet*, University of Nebraska Press, 1985.

[3] Benjamin Hawkins to Big Warrior, Little Prince and other Chiefs, June 16, 1814, *American State Papers, Indian Affairs*, Volume 1, p. 845.

[4] *Savannah Republican*, Volume IX, Issue 151, December 17, 1811, p. 3; *Federal Republican*, December 20, 1811, p. 1; *Rhode-Island American,* Volume IV, Issue 22, December 31, 1811, p. 3; *Poulson's American Daily Advertiser*, Volume XL, Issue 10,944, December 23, 1811, p. 3; *Charleston Courier*, Volume IX, Issue 2,764, December 17, 1811, p. 3, etc.

Chapter Two

Holy Ground

LITTLE IS KNOWN OF THE LIFE OF MILLY FRANCIS during the year she lived at Holy Ground. The town bordered the Alabama River and spring-fed creeks flowed along its margins. She undoubtedly played on the banks of these with her older sister, Polly, and the other children of the village. Her mother taught the girls how to cook and prepare traditional meals, to make moccasins and dresses from deer hide and all of the things important for a young girl to know in her time and place.

She listened to the sermons and prophesies of her father and watched his followers dance the "Dance of the Indians of the Lakes." Crowds of people came to Holy Ground to hear the new Alabama Prophet speak and to witness the events taking place there. Milly's uncle, Samuel Moniac, remembered that Francis initially had only a small group of followers:

...It was not till about Christmas that any of our people began to dance the war dance. The Muscogees have not been used to dance before war but after. At that time about 40 of our people began this northern custom; and my brother in law Francis who also pretends to be a prophet, was at the head of them.[1]

As the Prophet Francis continued to preach to his slowly growing congregation, Milly and the other girls of Holy Ground played and went about the daily routines of their lives. The little settlement grew into a village and soon into a town of considerable size. The winter of 1812, meanwhile, became the spring of 1813.

Among the early converts of the Prophet was a chief of Wewocau known as the Little Warrior. He took a group of believers north that winter to hear the Shawnee Prophet in person and learn more about his plans for the future of the movement. Although there is no documented proof, his mission likely was carried out at the direction of the Prophet Francis.

Little Warrior and his followers arrived in the Midwest to find Tenskwatawa and Tecumseh now living on the shores of the Great Lakes. They arranged for the Creek delegation to travel across the lakes to meet with a British official in Canada. The British army had not yet moved into the region, so later claims that Little Warrior met with a British general are not correct. The earliest accounts of his journey, however, mention only that he met with an unidentified British official, and this is probably true.

The officer explained that war had erupted between the United States and Great Britain. He provided Little Warrior's party with some new arms and ammunition and told them to carry back to the Creek Nation instructions to stockpile arms and ammunition and await further instructions from the British. He also gave them a letter – early accounts describe it as a "packet" – of some sort, the contents of which have never been revealed. Little Warrior was told, however, that the letter contained instructions to Spanish officials on the Gulf Coast to provide arms and ammunition to the Creeks.

When the spring thaw began, the delegation started on its way back south. Its members had spent the winter listening to the exhortations of the Shawnee Prophet, who had altered his teachings from the early days of his movement as a result of William Henry Harrison's campaign against Prophet's Town and the Battle of Tippecanoe. The whites, he now taught, were not humans like the Indians, but were the spawn of evil and had crawled up from the sea. They should be exterminated or driven back to the sea from whence they came.

As Little Warrior and his party neared the Ohio River with these thoughts in mind, they heard a rumor that Tecumseh and Tenskwatawa had begun their war against the whites. Believing this rumor to be true, they crossed the Ohio and made their way through Kentucky to Tennessee where they struck a series of homes along the Duck River. Men, women and children were killed. A survivor, Mrs. Martha Crowley, was taken prisoner and carried south into Alabama where she was rescued by the trader George S. Gaines.

The attacks on the Duck River outraged the whites and Colonel Hawkins demanded that the Big Warrior and Little Prince see that justice was done against those responsible for the slaughter. Hawkins, who at this time had heard little of the doings at Holy Ground and regarded the Alabama Prophet as a minor nuisance, did not foresee that by demanding justice for the murders in Tennessee, he was giving Francis the opportunity he needed to expand his movement to the entire Creek Nation.

The Big Warrior, meanwhile, tried to calm the American agent by assuring him that the Creeks had no intention of going to war against the whites:

> ...[Y]ou think that we lean to the Shawanee tribes, because you saw Tecumseh and his party dance in our square, around our fire, and some of our people believed their foolish talks. It is true, they have punished white people, and we take their lives to pay, according to law. Our old chiefs and fathers have been fooled by the British. We are not a-going to follow their steps. You need not be jealous that we will take up arms against the United States: we mean to kill all of our red people that spill the blood of our white friends. If all of the nations was a-going to make war on the white people, we would tell you that we wanted war, and not keep it as a secret; but we don't want war. The young warriors is a making of laws, the more mischief is done the more force to punish.[2]

In the traditional Creek way, the Big Warrior and other leading chiefs sent out execution squads to kill Little Warrior and his followers. The Coweta chief William McIntosh headed the effort. Little Warrior and his adherents were located, surrounded and killed. They fought back with great ferocity, yelling out the details of what they had done and showing no fear of death or of the members of the execution squads. Only one young boy was spared.

As McIntosh and his warriors tracked down and killed the members of Little Warrior's party, the United States suddenly seized the Spanish port of Mobile. The Americans claimed it was part of the Louisiana Purchase, which they said extended as far east as the Perdido River. The Spanish, however, claimed that their territory extended as far west as the Mississippi River. A group of revolutionaries had thrown the Spanish out of Baton Rouge in 1810 and declared the independence of the Republic of West Florida. They planned eventually to march east across West Florida, which then included parts of the modern states of Louisiana, Mississippi and Alabama, take Mobile and lay siege to Pensacola. They claimed the territory as their own, but the United States intervened by invading the short-lived republic in 1810. In April 1813, U.S. troops seized Mobile and forced the Spanish east of the Perdido River.

This move infuriated the Spanish governor in Pensacola, who feared that his city would be the next target. He sent a courier to the Upper Creeks requesting that they come down to Pensacola to receive arms and ammunition so they could assist in holding back the Americans. He calmed somewhat when the U.S. Army did not continue to advance and dispatched a second messenger to recall his courier, but it was too late. News already had arrived among the Upper Creeks that supplies for war could be obtained in Pensacola.

The Prophet Francis was alarmed by the seizure of Mobile and pointed out to his adherents that it was proof of his warning that the whites intended to surround and crush the Creek nation. In addition, he was outraged that the traditional chiefs had authorized the execution of Little Warrior's party. Hundreds of new converts flooded to Holy Ground in the wake of the killings. New prophets were made and the number of chiefs and warriors dancing the "Dance of the Indians of the Lake" grew from 40 to more than 1,000. In the traditional symbol of war, Francis raised a red war club at Holy Ground. It was this action that gave his followers the name by which they are remembered today, Red Sticks.

The war declared by the Prophet Francis was not against the whites, but against the traditional leaders of the Creek Nation. He meant to wipe out the Big Warrior, the Little Prince, William McIntosh and the other allies of Colonel Hawkins. The old interpreter Alexander Cornells was to be killed and then war parties would either kill or drive away Hawkins himself. Power would be concentrated into the hands of the Prophet and his followers and the Creek Nation would be unified and prepared to resist any further expansion by the whites.

As Milly and her friends watched, Holy Ground became a war capital. Parties of Red Stick warriors moved out to exact retribution on those who took part in the killings of Little Warrior and his followers. Her father drew great circles in the earth, declaring that they were spiritual barriers across which no white man could pass and live. The very ground itself would swallow him up.

To the shock of Colonel Hawkins, the Big Warrior and other supporters of the "plan of civilization," key leaders and towns of the Nation began to join the party of the Prophet. Peter McQueen, High-head Jim, Wewocau, the Tallassee King, Hoboheilthle Mico and others brought their entire villages into the growing Red

Stick movement. Stunned Creek leaders sent a strong demand to Francis that he produce proof of his miracles:

You are but a few Alabama people. You say that the Great Spirit visits you frequently; that he comes in the sun, and speaks to you; that the sun comes down just above your heads. Now, we want to see and hear what you say you have seen and heard. Let us have the same proof you have had, and we will believe what we see and hear. You have nothing to fear; the people who committed murders have suffered for their crimes, and there is an end of it.[3]

A prominent chief was selected to deliver the message to Holy Ground, but he did not survive the journey. Alexander Cornells and the Big Warrior accused Francis and his followers of killing him and his escorts, but they said otherwise:

The prophets denied to them they had killed the men charged on them, and said they made circles, into one of which, reserved for their prophet, they entered without leave, and were immediately seized with madness, and died. Hoboheilthle Micco, the old medal chief, he sent the denial of the murder by the prophets to Cussetah, and directed the Cussetah Micco to send it to all the towns below him, which he had done.[4]

The Big Warrior had been given proof of the power of the Prophet Francis. Shock waves reverberated through the Nation. The scalp of the messenger was sent up the Alabama River to a town where a second group of Red Sticks had congregated:

They went over to the house of Captain Isaacs, plundered, and burnt it. They executed two of his warriors who aided him to punish the murderers. After this, they gave out they would destroy Tuckaubatchee and Coweta, with every person in them; then kill Mr. Cornells, Tustunnuggee Thlucco, Mr. Hawkins, and the old chiefs who had taken his talks; after this war among themselves, they would be ready for the white people. They had power to destroy them by an earthquake, or by rendering the ground soft and miry, and thunder. The chiefs of Tuckaubatchee called in all their people, and sent for the neighboring towns. Seven of the nearest refused to oppose the prophets.[5]

The principal chiefs sent Alexander Cornells to the Lower Creek towns to solicit support, instructing him to proceed from there to the Agency on the Flint

River in Georgia to ask Colonel Hawkins for military help. He traveled at night surrounded by a squad of trusted warriors and managed to reach the Flint, arriving just ahead of a second messenger who brought an even more desperate call for help:

> *We have need of assistance, and we wish you, Colonel Hawkins, to assist us, by joining the white warriors with ours. Yours can come the post road opposite to us; we will join them, go with our forces united, march on both sides of the Alabama, and put an end to these hatchers of war and mischief. By showing them they are both feeble and ignorant, they will be crushed; as neither thunder, quagmire, or the sun, will come to their aid. They can soon be conquered, and those who support them at the lakes, be disappointed in their hopes of war. If your troops are so situated you cannot send them, write to our friend the Governor of Georgia. We hope he will help us, and then we shall have peace. Making peace here in this way, is making peace for our white neighbors as well as for ourselves.[6]*

Cornells and the second messenger, Talmus Hadjo, reached Hawkins' headquarters at the same time as a lesser prophet named Captain Snake. Hearing their reports, he announced angrily that the Red Stick plan had been exposed. "The prophets of Alabama had begun prematurely," he told Hawkins. "They were to go on with their magic until Tecumseh arrived, who was to put the plan in motion, and he would come when his friends the British were ready for him."[7]

Hawkins immediately send 11 rifles, 30 pounds of powder and a corresponding amount of shot to Cusseta, then headed for Milledgeville to discuss the situation with Governor Peter Early. A dispatch was sent by courier to John Armstrong, the Secretary of War.

As these events were taking place in Georgia, warriors from Holy Ground destroyed the town of Hatchechubbau and its detached settlements because its inhabitants had refused to join their party. The traditional chiefs sent two of their greatest men, Tuskeenohoau of Cusseta and Atchau Hadjo of Coweta to try to reason with Hoboheilthle Mico of Tallassee:

> *...[T]he old man rejected everything, declared his determination to persevere until he destroyed all who aided and assisted to put the murderers to death. He looked on them as people of the United States. He would march from Tuckaubatchee to Coweta, destroy all of them, and move on for the white people, and would not stop till he had marched to Ogeechee. There he would pause and*

rest, then put off for the sea coast. All north of this line of march would be destroyed by the British. He had been plotting this secretly for some time, and now having brought it to bear, he was determined not to stop. He had his bows, his arrows, and war clubs, and with the magic powers, aided by the British and Shawanese, who were now coming from the northwest, and were now more than half way to him, he was able to crush the Americans, and would do it.[8]

News had reached the Creek Agency that Peter McQueen, the war chief of Tallassee, had joined the Red Sticks and was on his way to Pensacola to obtain arms and ammunition from the Spanish. Groups from each village allied with the Prophet Francis were delegated to join him and in all some 300 men united with McQueen as he made his way south. Among these was a group headed by the Prophet High-Head Jim. While en route, Jim ran into Milly's uncle, Samuel Moniac, who had just arrived at his home on the Federal Road:

...An Indian came to me who goes by the name of High Headed Jim, and who I [learned] had been appointed to head a party sent from the Auttacee Town [i.e. Autossee on the Tallapoose, on a trip to Pensacola. He shook hands with me & immediately began to tremble & jerk in every part of his frame, and the very calves of his legs would be convulsed, and he would get entirely out of breath with the agitation. This Practice was introduced in May & June last by the prophet Francis who says that he was so instructed by the Spirit.[9]

Jim demanded that Moniac state plans for the future. The mestizo trader and farmer replied that he would sell his property to buy ammunition and then join the Red Sticks. By this ruse he saved his life, for the Red Sticks were putting to death all who opposed them:

...He then told me that they were going down to Pensacola, to get ammunition, and that they had got a letter from a British General, which would enable them to receive ammunition from the Governor. That it had been given to the Little Warrior & saved by his nephew when he was killed and sent down to Francis. . .He said that they were going to make a general attack on the American settlements, that the Indians on the waters of the Coose & Tallapoose & on the Black Warrior were to attack the settlements on the Tombigby & Alabama, particularly the Tensaw and Fork settlements. That the Creek Indians bordering on the Cherokees were to attack the people of Tennessee & that the Seminoles & Lower Creeks were to attack the Georgians. – That the Choctaws had also joined

17

them and were to attack the Mississippi Settlements. That the attack was to be made at the same time in all places when they got furnished with ammunition.[10]

Just as Moniac appeared at St. Stephens on the Tombigbee River to warn the whites, a message also arrived from the Choctaw chief Mushulatuba. It carried news that at least 80 of his warriors had joined the Prophet. The rest of the nation, he reported, was content to remain neutral.[11]

The power of the moment was clearly on the side of the Prophet Francis. White and mestizo residents on the fringes of the Nation began to "fort themselves in." This old expression meant that they were building log stockades around selected homes and gathering there for their own safety. Some 20 of these forts were built from the Tensaw settlement up through the forks of the Alabama and Tombigbee Rivers. The best known of these was Fort Mims at Tensaw. The association of the mestizo leader Dixon Bailey with this stockade assured its doom.

Milly Francis at this time was around 10 years old. Like other followers of her father, she likely believed that Holy Ground was a place of safety, protected by magic and the Master of Life from attack. The town had grown to include more than 200 houses and its total population numbered into the thousands. It must have been an exciting time for the young girl with so many people coming and going, the nightly dances in the square and the war whoops of Red Stick warriors as they arrived bearing the scalps of those who had opposed them.

Peter McQueen reached Pensacola where, after a tense few days, he received 1,000 pounds of powder and a corresponding amount of shot from Governor Mateo Gonzales Manrique. Spies brought news of this to the white settlements above Mobile and near panic erupted. Colonel James Caller ordered out the local militia and – without waiting for orders from higher authorities – set out to intercept McQueen's force as it returned from Pensacola to Holy Ground. Harry Toulmin, the new Federal judge for the Mobile region, supported the move but feared that it would not succeed:

I feel much anxiety about the issue of their enterprize. I have never approved of voluntary expeditions undertaken without the express authority of the government: but in this case our existence seems to depend on our promptitude. We know, without the shadow of a doubt, what are the intentions of the Indians. They will presently fall upon us in various quarters, and where we may be least prepared for them. They are now arraying themselves for the purpose. This is the moment, therefore, to baulk their cruel and most unjust and unprovoked aggression. Were we to wait for instructions from the general government, or even from the territorial executive, the whole of our frontier may be stained with blood before we had the power to check its effusion. . .It seemed justifiable, therefore, that attempts should be made by our citizens, without authority expressly given, to intercept and disarm the hostile Indians on their way from Pensacola. It is a case of imperious necessity – the step is required by a regard to self-preservation: but I doubt the result. I fear that they will not fall in with the Indians, or any considerable body of them; and if they do, I fear that the Indians, more skilled in the art of war, will be too well prepared to receive them.[12]

Judge Toulmin mentioned in his dispatch that among the men who turned out to intercept McQueen was a party of mestizo Creeks headed by Dixon Bailey. His involvement on the side of the whites made him a special enemy of the Prophet Francis and a target for his outrage.[13]

The judge had no way of knowing it when he wrote his dispatch, but the fatal Battle of Burnt Corn Creek already had taken place. With a force of around 180 men, including Dixon Bailey and his followers, Colonel Caller located McQueen's party eating their noon meal at a spring on the west side of Burnt Corn Creek. Arraying his men atop a semi-circular low ridge that surrounded the spring, he ordered a charge on McQueen's unsuspecting warriors:

Never was an enterprise more miserably managed. The officers, I mean the field officers, were totally inadequate both as to skill & courage for such an enterprize. The men in consequence of personal timidity and blundering orders, were presently thrown into confusion. Two-thirds of them fled, and the remainder sustained the conflict nearly two hours, and many of those in consequence of their perseverance lost their horses. The Indians lost about 200 lbs. of powder and some other articles – but our loss in horses, saddles, &c. was much more considerable. The present of the Spanish Gov. to M'Queen and his party amounted to about $2000, not less than 20 barrels of flour, 25 of corn, 50 blankets, a quantity of knives, razors, scissors, and about 1000lbs. of powder with a proportionate quantity of lead.[14]

The Battle of Burnt Corn Creek was a disaster for the whites. Only one Creek warrior was killed, although a slave fighting alongside the Red Sticks also died. Two whites were killed and 10 wounded. McQueen, however, had defeated an organized American military force and driven it from the battlefield. He lost 200 pounds of his powder but saved 800 pounds of powder and was able to capture both horses and weapons.

News of the Red Stick victory spread like lightening across the Nation. Colonel Hawkins heard about it within days. The scalps of the two white men killed were sent through the various towns for all to see, proof that the whites had attacked the Creeks without provocation. Hundreds of heretofore neutral warriors now joined the Prophet's party. The settlers of the Mississippi Territory had brought disaster on themselves. And they knew it:

Some of the most intelligent persons connected with the Creek nation, who have visited me today, and who have suffered much from the hostile proceedings of their countrymen, are of opinion that between two and three thousand warriors are now in arms against the United States. Ammunition is scarce – but without extraordinary vigilance on our part, they will obtain supplies. The Muscogee Prophet, however, tells them that guns are needless; that God will fight for them; and that on their first appearance on the field of battle, their enemies will be struck with a fire from Heaven, and be destroyed or dispersed. The issue of the skirmish a few days since, and the unaccountable panic which struck our leaders on that occasion, will give, indeed, to these dreams the stamp of prophetical authenticity.[15]

News of the Battle of Burnt Corn Creek electrified Holy Ground. Milly Francis undoubtedly watched as her father met with his principal prophets and war leaders to decide upon a course of action. That they would retaliate was clear, but where to strike was a matter of some debate. The Prophet favored an immediate move on the Big Warrior and other principal chiefs, who had retreated to Coweta with the warriors they were able to assemble. The families of those killed and wounded in the battle, however, demanded blood atonement from those responsible. Dixon Bailey drew their particular ire.

Creek belief held that a slain warrior could not go to his eternal reward until his death was avenged. The families demanded that Fort Mims, where many of those involved in the Burnt Corn attack were sheltered, be the target for their revenge. The Prophet Francis consulted with William Weatherford and other leading warriors and decided to bend to the will of the families. Fort Mims would be the target.

Milly Francis watched as her father led hundreds of warriors out of the town to begin the march on Fort Mims. Messengers were dispatched to allied towns and the size of the strike force grew as it advanced. By the time it neared the fort in late August, it included more than 700 warriors.

The role of the Prophet Francis in the attack on Fort Mims is one of the great mysteries of the Creek War of 1813-1814. He was the undisputed leader of the Red Sticks at the time and it is known that he led smaller war parties against settlements in the forks of the Alabama and Tombigbee Rivers a few days later. Most writers have accepted frontier tradition that Francis was not present at Fort Mims and that the Red Stick forces there were led by William Weatherford. The Prophet himself, however, told an English officer the following year that he was at Fort Mims in person. "Francis told me that while he was attacking Fort Mims the blacks were the first in," wrote Lieutenant Colonel Edward Nicolls on August 12, 1814, "and I have one man who killed seven Americans in that affair."[16]

As the wives and children of Holy Ground and the other Red Stick villages – Milly Francis among them – waited for news, the Red Stick warriors attacked Fort Mims at 11 a.m. on August 30, 1813. The gate of the fort had been left open and slaves had even been whipped for giving "false reports" that they had seen Creek warriors in the vicinity. The men of Fort Mims were sitting in two circles discussing what they might do if actually attacked when the shot of a sentry was fired and the war cry of the Red Sticks erupted outside their walls. The charging warriors were within 30 steps of the gate before they were discovered.

The battle lasted for hours, but by the time darkness descended, Fort Mims had fallen. To this day no one knows how many men, women and children died within its walls. A burial party later located and interred nearly 250 whites and another 100 "Indians." It is unknown whether the "Indians" mentioned in the report were Red Sticks or the Creek mestizos who had come into the fort along with Dixon Bailey. The later probability is most likely. Dixon Bailey fought with courageous fury, but in the end he died alongside his white friends. Many of the women and children of Fort Mims burned to death in the upper floor of Samuel Mims' house while the blood-covered Red Sticks danced in celebration to the sound of their screams.

---

[1] Samuel Moniac, "The Deposition of Samuel Manac," August 2, 1813, SPR 26, Alabama Department of Archives and History.
[2] Big Warrior, Alex. Cornells and William McIntosh to Benjamin Hawkins, April 26, 1813, ASPIA, Volume I, p. 841.

[3] Alexander Cornells, Interpreter, to Benjamin Hawkins, June 22, 1813, ASPIA, Volume I, pp. 845-846.

[4] *Ibid.*

[5] *Ibid.*

[6] *Ibid.*, Addendum dated June 23, 1814.

[7] *Ibid.*

[8] Talosee Fixico, runner from Tuckabatchee, to Benjamin Hawkins, July 5, 1813, ASPIA, Volume 1, p. 847.

[9] Samuel Moniac, "The Deposition of Samuel Manac," August 2, 1813, SPR 26, Alabama Department of Archives and History.

[10] *Ibid.*

[11] Mushulatuba to George S. Gaines, July 15, 1813, published in the Richmond Enquirer, September 7, 1813, p. 2.

[12] Hon. Harry Toulmin, July 29, 1813, published in the Universal Gazette, Volume XI, Issue 819, September 9, 1813, p 4.

[13] *Ibid.*

[14] A Respectable Gentleman [Harry Toulmin] to Col. Benjamin Hawkins, August 13, 1813, published in the Daily National Intelligencer, Volume I, Issue 218, September 13, 1813, p. 3.

[15] Harry Toulmin, August 2, 1813, published in the Universal Gazette, VolumeXI, Issue 819, September 9, 1813, p. 4.

[16] Lt. Col. Edward Nicolls to Adm. Alexander Cochrane, August 12, 1814, CP, 2328, pp. 59-62.

Alabama River near Selma, Alabama

Comet of 1811 (#3)

Tecumseh in British Uniform

Tenskwatawa ("Open Door"), the Shawnee Prophet

Josiah Francis, the Creek Prophet (self portrait)

19th Century drawing of the New Madrid Earthquake, 1811-1812

Holy Ground Battlefield Park near White Hall, Alabama

Jim Boy (High-Head Jim), a Creek Prophet and follower of Josiah Francis

Chapter Three

Attack on the Prophet's Town

BY THE FALL OF 1813, MILLY FRANCIS HAD WITNESSED some of the most significant events in American history. She had seen the Comet of 1811 and felt the ground shake beneath her feet during the New Madrid earthquakes. With her own eyes she had observed the visit of Tecumseh to the Creek Nation and the rise of her father as the Alabama Prophet. She saw William Weatherford following his conversion to her father's religion and in early September she watched as the victorious Red Sticks returned from Fort Mims.

The warriors brought back mountains of supplies and desperately needed food for the large population that had concentrated at Holy Ground. The Prophet's admonition to destroy livestock and crops associated with the whites had caused hunger to descend on the towns of the Red Sticks, but through the fall of Fort Mims and evacuation of the downriver farms and plantations, the Master of Breath had provided for his followers.

There were prisoners from Fort Mims. The women and children captured there were sent on to Wewocau, but the African slaves were kept at Holy Ground. Some joined the Prophet's cause, but those who did not were executed during the frenzied celebrations that followed. Whether Milly observed any of these killings is not known, but she undoubtedly saw the large red pole covered with scalps that the victorious warriors raised on the square of the town. The hair of men, women and children adorned the grisly monument.

Milly's father was at the height of his power. In taking Fort Mims, the Red Sticks had done what no one thought possible. Not since the days of the Yamassee War of the early 1700s had the Creeks achieved such a dramatic victory over the whites. It came at great cost – well over 100 Red Sticks had been killed and wounded – but was such a tremendous success that even more Creeks joined the Prophet's party. Panic gripped whites along the borders of the nation. Smaller forts were evacuated and women and children made a desperate night movement from the U.S. Army cantonment at Mt. Vernon, Alabama, to the safety of Mobile.

Even there they were not safe. Flush with their victory over the whites at Fort Mims, the Red Sticks made an offer to the Spanish governor in Pensacola to retake or destroy Mobile for the King. He politely declined.

On a broader scale, however, the victory at Fort Mims sealed the doom of the Prophet Francis and the Red Stick movement. As word reached Natchez, Nashville, Milledgeville and finally Washington, D.C., the southern states blazed with fury. Armies formed in Tennessee, Georgia and the Mississippi Territory and a strategy was devised for all three to drive into the Creek Nation from different directions at the same time. They would meet at the sacred Hickory Ground where the Coosa and Tallapoosa Rivers united to form the Alabama. The Prophet and his followers knew neither the extent of these preparations nor the determination of the American leaders now arrayed against them.

From the north, Governor Willie Blount of Tennessee ordered Major General Andrew Jackson into the field with thousands of volunteers and militia. Old Hickory drove south into the northern edge of the Nation and despite problems created by supply shortages and inexperienced troops, devastated large forces of Red Sticks at the Battles of Tallushatchee and Talladega. By the army's count, nearly 500 Red Stick warriors were killed in the fighting. A column from Jackson's army also penetrated the towns on the Black Warrior River, leveling everything in its path. Although he was then an unknown soldier from Tennessee, at least one member of this latter detachment was destined for fame. His name was David Crockett.

From the east, General John Floyd moved from the frontier of Georgia into the Lower Creek towns. After halting to build a supply depot named Fort Mitchell, Floyd drove all the way to the Tallapoosa River and struck the noted Red Stick town of Autossee (Atasi). Guided by Alabama's first Jewish settler, Abraham Mordecai, the Georgia army hit Autossee at sunrise on November 29,

1813. The battle was fierce, but ended in bloody disaster for the Red Sticks. Two hundred were reported killed.

Between them, the Tennessee and Georgia armies had killed an estimated 700 Red Stick warriors and destroyed town after town loyal to the Prophet. Then in December, the Mississippi army of Brigadier General Ferdinand L. Claiborne began its march on Holy Ground. The great test of the power of the Prophet was at hand.

Prior to beginning his campaign, Claiborne had advanced 85 miles up the Alabama River from his previous headquarters at Fort Stoddert and built a new stockade - Fort Claiborne - that he named for himself. With this fort secure, the general directed his force up the west side of the Alabama for Holy Ground. The march began on December 13, 1813:

...When I had marched about 30 miles, I was informed that we were within 30 miles of a considerable town, called Eccanachaca (or Holy Ground) where the Indians from the neighboring villages had assembled in considerable force – where Witherford, who has made himself conspicuous by his depredations on our frontiers, and by the massacre at fort Mimms and where Josiah Francis, a principal prophet, resided.[1]

The "Witherford" mentioned in Claiborne's letter was, of course, William Weatherford. Moving to within 30 miles of Holy Ground, Claiborne halted his army while the men built another stockade to protect his baggage and sick. This stockade was named Fort Deposit and it stood near today's town of the the same name.

It took about one week for the soldiers to finish Fort Deposit and for Claiborne to fend off the desire expressed by some to turn back. Supply shortages and expiring enlistments were discouraging many of his officers and men. Despite such obstacles, the general pushed forward on the morning of December 22, 1813, rapidly closing the distance between his army and Holy Ground.[2]

It is remarkable that Claiborne marched his army to within 30 miles of Holy Ground and hovered there for one full week building a stockade without ever being detected by Red Stick scouts. Life went on as normal in the town, where the followers of the Prophet believed they were safe and secure behind the magic circles he had drawn in the dirt. Milly and the other members of his family were going about their daily routines even as the Mississippi army approached.

That all changed on the morning of December 23rd. Claiborne was now within striking distance of Holy Ground and began to shift his army from column formation into a line of battle:

On the morning of the 23d, when near the town, my disposition for the attack was made. I marched in three columns. The right composed of volunteers commanded by colonel Carson; the left consisted of militia, and a party of Chactaws, commanded by major Smoot, of militia; and the centre, being part of the 3d U.S. regiment of infantry and mounted riflemen, under lt. col. Russel. With this column I myself marched; having ordered Lester's guards and Wills' troop of dragoons to act as a corps of reserve.[3]

As the soldiers struggled noisily through the ravines and swamps that surrounded Holy Ground, they were detected by Red Stick sentries. Chaos erupted in the village. Despite the presence of warriors and the magical protection with which he had surrounded the town, Francis wisely ordered the evacuation of the women and children. As William Weatherford and other chiefs led warriors forward to fight Claiborne's soldiers, Milly Francis and other noncombatants were rushed down the bluff to canoes. Just a 10 year old girl at the time, she grabbed what she could and hurried with her mother and siblings into a canoe and pushed off for the opposite shore. Their goal was to put the Alabama River between them and the American army and then to get as far away as possible. Like other evacuees from Holy Ground, Milly and her family escaped with little more than the clothes on their backs. Behind them, they could hear gunfire erupt as Weatherford and his outnumbered warriors tried to hold back Claiborne's attack:

...About noon the right column, composed of twelve months' volunteers, commanded by Col. Joseph Carson, came in view of the town, called Eccanachaca, (or Holy Ground,) and was immediately vigorously attacked by the enemy, who were apprized of our approach, and had chosen their field of action.

Before the centre, commanded by Lieut. Col. Russell, with a part of the 3d regiment of United States' infantry and mounted militia riflemen, or the left column, which was composed of militia and a party of Choctaws under Pushautaha, commanded by Major Smoot, of militia, who were ordered to charge, could come generally into action, the enemy were repulsed and were flying in all directions, many of them casting away their arms.

Thirty of the enemy were killed, and judging from every appearance many were wounded. The loss on our part was one corporal killed, and one ensign, two sergeants, one corporal and two privates wounded.[4]

The Holy Ground of the Prophet Josiah Francis had fallen. As the battle deteriorated and the Red Stick warriors scattered in all directions, one of the most remarkable events of the Creek War took place. Pursued by U.S. troops, William Weatherford mounted his horse – Arrow - and rode to the bluff overlooking the Alabama River. Turning both left and right looking for a route of escape, he found every possible avenue blocked by converging soldiers. With no other option left, he turned back from the edge of the bluff for some distance, then spun his horse about and rode full speed for the crest. As the amazed soldiers watched, Weatherford put spurs to Arrow and the horse galloped at full speed off the top of the bluff. Rider and horse seemed suspended in air as they arched far out over the water before splashing down into the cold Alabama. Both went completely underwater when they hit the river, but Arrow soon emerged with Weatherford still clinging to his back. They reached the other side and members of Claiborne's army watched from the bluff as the "Red Eagle" of Alabama legend dismounted, shook the water from his blanket and looked back at them before remounting Arrow and riding away.

Weatherford's Leap remains a popular Alabama legend to this day and, although it has been much debated and many alternate theories offered, no one has ever been able to prove that it did not happen. Even though he was defeated, William Weatherford lives on in Southern memory, while General Claiborne – the victor of the Battle of Holy Ground – is all but forgotten.

Having crossed the Alabama River even as the Americans were beginning their attack, it is possible that Milly Francis was among the Creeks who witnessed Weatherford's Leap from the opposite shore. If so, it must have ranked in her mind alongside the Comet of 1811, the earthquakes and seeing Tecumseh in person in the annals of her memory.

The Prophet Francis also escaped from Holy Ground and soon joined his family on the opposite shore. His magic had failed. Fierce battles were still to come, but for many of the Red Stick warriors, the Master of Life was no longer with them. William Weatherford soon broke with the Prophet and his followers and the Hillabee towns, despite a brutal massacre carried out by Tennessee troops not under Jackson's command, made peace with the whites.

As the dreams of Josiah Francis died across the river from Holy Ground, the American troops took stock of their situation:

A pursuit was immediately ordered; but from the nature of the country, nothing was effected. The town was nearly surrounded by swamps and deep ravines, which rendered our approach difficult, and facilitated the escape of the enemy. In the town we found a large quantity of provisions and immense property of various kinds, which the enemy, flying precipitately were obliged to leave behind, and which, together with two hundred homes, were destroyed. They had barely time to remove their women and children across the Alabama, which runs near where the town stood.[5]

Exactly where Milly and her family went after the Battle of Holy Ground is not clear. Some writers have asserted that the Prophet fled the Creek Nation in disgrace and made his way to Pensacola to seek the protection of the Spanish. Other sources, however, are clear that he remained in the Nation and continued to fight the oncoming American armies.

It is known that Francis and Peter McQueen helped lead the surprise attack on General Floyd's army at Calabee Creek in January 1814, killing 22 men of the Georgia army and wounding 150. One day later they took part in the devastating attack that shattered the rear of Andrew Jackson's army at Enitichopco. Had it not been for the personal courage and commanding presence of "Old Hickory" himself, the Tennessee army might well have been destroyed.

The Prophet's association with Peter McQueen in these battles suggests that he might have gone to Tallassee or that both had joined the growing Red Stick force at Tohopeka (Horseshoe Bend). At some point in February or early March, however, the reconsolidated Red Stick force divided, with Menawa remaining in command at Tohopeka while Francis, McQueen and others went to Hoithlewaulee and the Hickory Ground. The Prophet's family – including Milly – probably accompanied him on these various moves.

The end came on March 27, 1814, when Jackson attacked the fortified Red Stick town at Tohopeka. After a brutal engagement in which warriors fought to the death rather than surrender, the American flag floated over the bloody field of the Battle of Horseshoe Bend. The Georgia army and additional regulars soon arrived, but by the time the combined U.S. force could advance on Hoithlewaulee and the Hickory Ground, the large Red Stick force that had assembled there under Francis and McQueen was gone. As the victorious Americans built Fort Jackson in the very heart of the Creek Nation, the surviving Red Sticks either surrendered or began a desperate flight for Spanish Florida.

[1] Brig. Gen. Ferdinand L. Claiborne to Gov. Willie Blount, January 1, 1814, published in the Ohio Republican, Volume I, Issue 38, p. 2. (February 12, 1814).

[2] *Ibid.*

[3] *Ibid.*

[4] *Ibid.*

[5] *Ibid.*

Chapter Four

Escape to Florida

THE DESTRUCTION OF MENAWA'S ARMY AT HORSESHOE BEND was the breaking point for the Red Stick movement in Creek Nation. Their strongest major army, protected by their strongest fortification, had fallen. The bodies of more than 500 warriors littered the field, where their bones would be seen for decades to come.

The evacuation of Hoithlewaulee and the Hickory Ground in the wake of the disaster at Horseshoe Bend precipitated a general flight of surviving Red Stick warriors and their families for Spanish Florida. Many surrendered to the American army as Jackson pushed on to the site of the old French settlement of Fort Toulouse, William Weatherford among them. Peter McQueen was taken prisoner by U.S. troops, but managed to escape. Josiah Francis eluded capture and fled south with his wife and children, hoping to escape death at the hands of Andrew Jackson.

Milly Francis was now around 11 years old and once again had become a refugee. The fleeing Red Sticks had few if any supplies and untold numbers collapsed from starvation. How well the Prophet was able to provide even for his own family at this time is not known. A British officer who saw him and other Red Stick leaders after they reached Florida described them as "skin and bones."

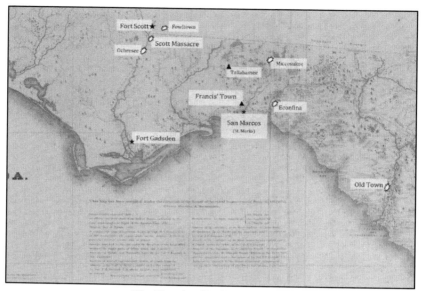

The Florida of Milly Francis

Making matters worse, detachments of American troops, Choctaw warriors and McIntosh's Creeks pursued them in their flight. Even their former ally, William Weatherford, was now an enemy to them:

At the head of the red warriors I soon placed the famous Bill Weatherford (a half breed) of whose integrity, and great usefulness to me during the whole of this expedition, I cannot speak in too high terms, and of whom, I am induced to believe, evil report has said more than he deserves. He does not deny that he fought, and that he fought desperately too; but he solemnly avers that he never knowingly or intentionally hurt, still less killed, a woman or child during the war.[1]

With Weatherford's help, Colonel J.A. Pearson – who penned the above while in pursuit of the Red Sticks – captured a number of refugees from the Prophet's base in the Alabama towns. Among these were the Coosada (Coushatta) King, the Tawasa chief Tibitsee and the Cahaba chief Hamohoee along with 69 warriors and 137 women and children. Another 339 men, women and children were found in the swamps along the Alabama River below the destroyed site of Holy Ground and convinced to surrender. Among these were found 16 African women and children, slaves who had been captured by the Red Sticks at Fort

Mims the previous August. Their husbands and fathers, they reported, had been executed.[2]

Weatherford and Graham captured the lesser Alabama prophet Naututge and made arrangements for the surrender of Paddy Walsh, but they were not able to get their hands on Josiah Francis. Even so, Graham was comfortable in proclaiming an end to the "disturbances" caused by the Prophet:

...[Y]ou may calculate on my bringing to Fort Jackson, besides the 339 prisoners now in my possession, two Alabama prophets, and near or quite 200 prisoners, making a total of more than 500 during this expedition; which I think, will pretty well settle the hostile party on the Alabama. In this number are about 200 warriors, stout, likely young men, with fierce intelligence countenances and a manly deportment. This expedition will fritter down the hostile party still out in so inconsiderable a number, that no great mischief need be apprehended from them in my opinion.[3]

Francis and his followers avoided their pursuers by crossing overland to the basin of the Conecuh River. He followed this stream to the Escambia River and Spanish Florida. By June 1814 he was in Pensacola and contemporary reports from that city indicated that he and other Red Stick leaders had secreted their families in the swamps of the Conecuh. These noncombatants likely included Milly, her siblings and her mother. The conditions under which they lived at this time were inconceivable. They had neither food nor conveniences of any kind. The warriors left to protect them had little if any ammunition for their rifles and muskets and used bows and arrows to bring down what game they could find. Untold numbers died of hunger and disease, their bones lost to time in the swamps of the Conecuh River.

Newspapers of the day went so far as to announce the death of the Prophet Francis, incorrect reporting that he had been killed in a confrontation with Col. Gilbert Russell's troops. Within a couple of weeks, however, they began to backtrack from the story:

...[T]hey have also in confinement, the old Tallassee or Sam King, who it is said was killed at the battle of Ottossee by the Georgia troops under the command of Gen. Floyd; it appears since, it was his brother who was killed, and that it was owing to the mistake of the friendly Indians, in supposing him to be the old Tame King. The remainder of the hostile Indians have fled towards Pensacola, with M'Queen and Francis, their principal leaders, at their head. We have no

confirmation of the recent report of Colonel Russell, of the 3d U.S. Reft. Having met them on their route, and destroyed a number....[4]

American troops along with war parties of Choctaws and Creeks continued to pursue the Red Sticks. McQueen and Francis shifted the location of their people, bringing them down across the line into Florida and secreting them in camps along the Yellow Water and Choctawhatchee Rivers. They escaped just ahead of American raiding parties that soon penetrated the valley of the Conecuh and Escambia Rivers.

Desperate to obtain supplies and provisions, Francis and McQueen went to Pensacola where Governor Mateo Gonzales Manrique did what he could to help them. He did not have available the sheer volume of supplies needed to relieve the starving Red Stick warriors and families, but help soon came from another source. The British had finally arrived in Spanish Florida.

Captain Hugh Pigot and Lieutenant David Hope of the Royal Navy reached Apalachicola Bay on May 11, 1814, with His Majesty's Ships *Orpheus* and *Shelbourne*. On board were supplies of food, ammunition, blankets and an arsenal of 2,000 new British muskets. Acting Lieutenant George Woodbine of the Royal Marines was assigned to organize and train Creek and Seminole recruits as part of an auxiliary force that would support British operations along the Gulf Coast. His instructions were to make contact with chiefs in the region of the Apalachicola and to establish a new fort in the vicinity.[5]

Woodbine located several chiefs and they came aboard the vessels at Apalachicola Bay on May 20, 1814. On the next day, Corporal James Denny and Sergeant Samuel Smith of the Royal Marines went ashore to begin training the gathering chiefs and warriors in tactics for the use of small arms. A log storehouse was built on St. Vincent Island and the British began to distribute supplies and ammunition to the Indians.[6]

Woodbine soon moved his effort up the lower Apalachicola to the vicinity of the John Forbes & Company store at Prospect Bluff. There, about 30 miles upstream from the bay, the British starting building a fort and storehouse. Reaching the bluff on May 25, Woodbine sent the Seminole chief Yellow Hair west to find Francis and McQueen.[7]

Yellow Hair's mission was a success. He located the refugee camps and learned that the two leaders had gone to Pensacola for supplies. Following them to the Spanish city, he notified Francis and McQueen of the British arrival on the Apalachicola and invited them to bring their people for supplies and assistance. They responded with a written plea for help:

Our case is really miserable and lamentable, driven from House and Home without Food and Clothes to cover our Bodies by disasters and an Enemy, who has sworn our ruin, and hovering about Pensacola and its Vicinity, where We can get no Assistance, as the Spanish Governor tells Us that it is scarsely able to support its Own Troops.[8]

Francis informed the British that despite the disaster that had befallen their movement, they had "determined to make no peace with the United States of America without the British government's consent."[9]

Once again the weary families began to move. The destination this time was the new British Post on the Apalachicola. The Prophet's family, Milly included, took part in this long walk. Her father boarded a schooner at Pensacola for fast transport to Apalachicola, but the warriors, women and children made their way on foot eastward across the Florida Panhandle. The exact route they followed is not known, but their journey took them across the Choctawhatchee and Chipola Rivers. When they reached Prospect Bluff, Francis was waiting for them as was McQueen, who had arrived with a few of his warriors on a second vessel. Although food was still not in plentiful supply, they had been saved. The British gave them fresh beef and barrels of flour while the upriver towns of Yellow Hair, Mulatto King, Thomas Perryman and William Perryman sent down corn and any other supplies they could spare to relieve the suffering of the refugees.

For Milly Francis, the arrival at the British Post must have been a moment of inexplicable thanksgiving. Hungry and suffering from the elements, with her clothing reduced to rags, she found herself in a place where white men and traditional chiefs came to assist her instead of attacking her as they had done on the Alabama. Lieutenant Colonel Edward Nicolls, who soon arrived to take command of the fort, provided some insight to the condition of the people in groups like the one in which Milly had arrived:

...[S]uch objects I never saw the like of, absolute skin and bone, but cheerfull and resolved to do their utmost against the common enemy. An old man told me, when I asked him how far it was to where the enemy were, and if he knew the way to lead me to them, he said it was seven days journey to them, that he could not miss the way for it was marked by the graves of his five children.[10]

41

How many innocent children died during the Red Stick flight to Florida will never be known. Milly and her older sister Polly somehow survived, as did their mother and other members of the family. Many of their friends and acquaintances, however, died along the way. The demon of war had unleased its greatest horrors on children and innocents.

---

[1] Col J.G. Pearson to Brig. Gen. Joseph Graham, June 1, 1814 (published in the *Raleigh Minerva*).

[2] *Ibid.*

[3] *Ibid.*

[4] Letter from a "gentleman in the Executive Department" at Milledgeville, GA to a resident of Alexandria, VA, published in the *Alexandria Gazette*, Volume XIV, Issue 4165, p. 3. (May 21, 1814).

[5] Sugden, p. 281.

[6] *Ibid.*

[7] *Ibid.*, pp. 281-282.

[8] Joshua Francis, Yaholloasaptko, Hopoyhisilyholla to British Commander at St. George's Island, June 9, 1814, CP, 2328, pp. 28-29.

[9] *Ibid.*

[10] Lt. Col. Edward Nicolls to Admiral Alexander Cochrane, August 12, 1814, CP 2328, pp. 59-61.

Chapter Five

Life among the Seminoles

THE PROPHET FRANCIS WAS A FIXTURE in the British service during the final year of the War of 1812, but little is known of the life of his daughter Milly during this time period. Most of the surviving families of the Red Sticks who fled to Florida made the long trek to Prospect Bluff where they were fed by the British. At the height of the operation, the villages surrounding the fort contained thousands of residents. Milly Francis was among them. It is not known whether she, her sister and her mother stayed there when the Prophet returned to Pensacola with Colonel Nicolls later in the summer, but it is known that many of the families made the journey back to the Spanish city.

With the acquiescence of Governor Mateo Gonzales Manrique, the British occupied Pensacola during the summer of 1814. They then violated the neutrality of Spain by using the old city as a base for an attack on Fort Bowyer, the U.S. fort that guarded the entrance to Mobile Bay. Headed by Captain William H. Percy of the Royal Navy, a squadron of four British warships landed a force of around 80 Royal Colonial Marines and 120 Red Stick Creek and Seminole warriors near present-day Gulf Shores. Twenty of the Marines then took up a position to block access to Mobile Point from Bon Secour while the rest of the land force marched west to the point and erected a battery in the sand dunes within range of the fort.

Colonel Nicolls was severely ill with dysentery at the time of the expedition and remained aboard the HMS *Hermes*, turning over command of the land forces to Captain Woodbine.

On September 15, 1814, Percy cleared for battle, formed his ships in line and closed on Fort Bowyer, which was held by Major William Lawrence and 120 men from the 2nd U.S. Infantry. Lawrence and his men watched as the British ships drew closer. The Americans opened fire at 4:20 p.m. The ships responded and the British land battery opened fire with a howitzer. Return fire from the fort quickly silenced the firing of the land battery, but the battle with the ships continued for almost three hours. The citizens and U.S. troops in Mobile could hear the firing of the cannon and waited with great apprehension. Few believed that the little fort could hold.

Like Fort McHenry at Baltimore had done just one day earlier, however, Fort Bowyer remained defiant. When the guns finally fell silent, the Star Spangled Banner still flew over the fort. Percy's flagship, the *Hermes*, had been shot to pieces and was abandoned after being set afire by her own crew. Despite his illness, Colonel Nicolls had taken part in the battle and suffered the loss of an eye when a wooden splinter was driven into it after an American cannonball struck the side of the ship. The magazine on the *Hermes* exploded at 10 p.m. and she went to the bottom just 600 yards offshore from Fort Bowyer.

Another of the British ships was severely damaged and what remained of the flotilla broke off the battle and limped back to Pensacola. The warriors and British Marines of the land force made their own way back to the Spanish city, doing considerable damage to the scattered homes along their route as they went. The Battle of Fort Bowyer had been a disaster for the British and a stunning victory for the Americans.[1]

The attack on Fort Bowyer and particularly the fact that it was launched from a supposedly neutral Spanish city infuriated Andrew Jackson and other officers of the U.S. Army. After praising Major Lawrence and his men for their gallant stand, the general concluded that Pensacola should be occupied and the British expelled. The American army formed near the ruins of Fort Mims and in November marched out for Pensacola.

Scouts brought news into the city that U.S. troops were on the move, prompting chaos and an angry confrontation between Colonel Nicolls and the Spanish governor who could not make up his mind as to whether he should accept British offers to help defend the city. Realizing that the governor's confusion had rendered the prospect of a successful defense improbable, Nicolls ordered that the Red Stick and Seminole women and children be evacuated.[2]

The operation to move the noncombatants out of harm's way began on November 3rd and continued for two days. Protected by the warriors who had concentrated at Pensacola, the woman and children were moved across the bay to a place of safety. Although conclusive proof is lacking, the probability is high that Milly Francis and the rest of the Prophet's family were among them. Milly was then around 11 years old and for at least the third time in her life, she had been forced to flee ahead of oncoming American troops. Even the anticipated sanctuary of Spanish Florida had proved to be unsafe.

As the families began the long walk back to the Apalachicola, Jackson's troops stormed Pensacola and seized control of the city. The British blew up Fort Barrancas and sailed out of the bay after threatening to level Pensacola with their guns but then deciding not to subject its citizens to artillery barrages. Jackson's troops arrived on the Barrancas heights in time to watch them sail away.

Having expelled the British, Jackson soon handed Pensacola back over to the Spanish and marched back to American territory. He was determined, however, to put an end to the Red Stick threat once and for all. From Fort Montgomery, a new U.S. post near Fort Mims, he ordered Major Uriah Blue of the 39th Infantry to take a large force of Choctaw warriors and Tennessee volunteers into West Florida to root out the Red Sticks and destroy the British Post on the Apalachicola. Among the Tennesseans in Blue's strike force was David Crockett.

As the warriors and their families – Milly Francis probably among them – made their way overland for the Apalachicola, Blue's column moved into Florida to pursue them. The Americans captured some Red Sticks and their families on the Escambia and Yellow Water Rivers then struck a large Red Stick camp on the Choctawhatchee. The inhabitants of the camp had evacuated ahead of the troops and the houses were empty when Blue and his men stormed the settlement.[3]

The Red Sticks, however, escaped and Major Blue, who had expected to capture supplies, now found his men facing starvation. Assessing the situation, he decided it would be impossible for him to continue on to the Apalachicola. With the Choctaw warriors, he fell back to the Escambia and Alabama while ordering the Tennesseeans to strike due north as fast as they could move for the American forts on the Tallapoosa. Both divisions suffered greatly from hunger, but eventually made their way to safety.[4]

The Red Sticks, Seminoles and families reached the Apalachicola and on November 22, 1814, Captain Robert Henry reported to Admiral Alexander

Cochrane that 1,100 warriors, 450 women and 755 children were at the post. Although she was not named, Milly Francis was one of the children.[5]

News of the severe terms exacted on the Creeks by the Treaty of Fort Jackson by this time had spread far and wide through the Creek Nation. Jackson had forced the Creeks to cede some 8,000,000 acres to the United States as reparations for the cost of the war. The ceded lands included the entire section of the Nation bordering Spanish Florida, including all of what is now Southeast Alabama and Southwest Georgia.

Many of the Creeks, including warriors who had allied with the United States during the war, were outraged by the severity of the terms. They felt punished even though they had supported and fought alongside American troops in putting down the Red Stick movement. Surviving Red Sticks still in the nation, meanwhile, realized that the Prophet had been right about white aims on their territory. Hundreds of warriors who just one year earlier had been in arms against each other began to make their way to the British Post on the Apalachicola. Five hundred new Creeks had arrived there from towns within the American lines in November alone.[6]

War material was plentiful at Prospect Bluff, but food and other supplies were not. Even so, the settlement formed by the British survived and grew. Warriors trained for combat while their families remained secure behind the protection of the heavy guns of the fort.

The fort became home to Milly Francis for the winter of 1814-1815. Based on a map drawn the following spring by Spanish surveyor Josef Pintado, the British Post was an extensive affair. An earthwork battery built in the shape of pointed angle or projection had been constructed on the edge of the low bluff where it projected slightly into the river. The heavy artillery, including naval 24-pounders, was mounted here. Directly to the rear of the battery was an octagonal citadel surrounded by a moat. Built of earth and massive timbers, it served as a magazine for the massive stockpile of arms brought to Prospect Bluff for use in supplying the warriors and African allies of the British. Stockades ran from the citadel to the river, connecting with the Apalachicola on each side of the battery to form a giant triangle.[7]

The interior of this triangle seems to have been reserved for military purposes, but on each side of it were the villages where the families of the British allies built houses. Milly Francis undoubtedly lived in one of these, her family given residence inside the compound due to her father's influential status.[8]

The entire affair was surrounded by a ditch and breastwork that took the form of a large rectangle, with bastions on the two inland corners. It was an extensive fortification but with their allies the British had enough men to defend it. In addition to the Red Stick and Seminole warriors congregating at the Bluff, Nicolls and Woodbine were forming and training companies of Colonial Marines from the Africans who came there both from Spanish Florida and the United States. Some were escaped slaves but many were free. Uniformed and equipped, they were given traditional British military instruction with both small arms and artillery.

This was the scene that Milly Francis saw taking place around her during the winter of 1814-1815. Once again she witnessed important figures and events that would play a significant role in American history. In addition to her father and Peter McQueen, she undoubtedly came to know Kenhajo (Cappachimico), the head chief of the massive Seminole town of Miccosukee; Garcon, the former slave of the Forbes company who became the Sergeant Major of the Colonial Marines battalion formed at the Bluff; Colonel Nicolls and Captain Woodbine as well as a variety of important Seminole and Creek chiefs.

By all indications, Nicolls and Woodbine admired their Creek, Seminole and black allies and came to know them as human beings. In his letters, Nicolls speaks of conversations with various chiefs including the Prophet Francis and of the suffering they and their families had experienced. Not all British officers, however, were so convinced of the humanity of their allies. Captain Edward Codrington, for example, described visits to the HMS *Tonnant* by several of his nation's new Creek and Seminole friends:

...I find I have not yet, however, mentioned to you the arrival of our magnanimous allies Kings Capichi and Hopsy (or Perriman), with their upper and second warriors, the Prophet Francis, Helis Hadjo, the ambassador from the Big Warrior, &c., &c. We had the honour of these Majestic Beasts dining with us two days in the 'Tonnant,' and we are to be disgusted with a similar honour here to-day.[9]

The King "Capichi" mentioned by Codrington was Kenhajo (Cappachimico) of Miccosukee while the "Hopsy (or Perriman)" was the mestizo chief Thomas Perryman who had fought for the British during the American Revolution. Despite their service to his country, Codrington obviously considered them as something less than human. In a letter to a relative dated December 14, 1814, he went on to describe the chiefs, Josiah Francis among them:

...All the body clothes they get they put on one over the other, except trowsers, which they consider as encumbrances it should seem in our way of using

them, and they therefore tie them round their waists for the present, in order to convert them into leggings hereafter. Some of them appeared in their own picturesque dresses at first, with the skin of a handsome plumed bird on the head and arms; the bird's beak pointing down the forehead, the wings over the ears, and the tail down the poll. But they are now all in hats (some cocked, gold-laced ones), and in jackets such as are worn by sergeants in the Guards, and they have now the appearance of dressed-up apes. . . .[10]

Codrington's account of the bird headdress is significant in that it is one of the only detailed accounts of the headgear often mentioned as having been worn by Red Stick prophets during the Creek War of 1813-1814. The prophets who animated Red Stick forces at the Battle of Horseshoe Bend wore headdresses made from birds, as did other prophets seen, captured or killed by American forces. The headdress described by Codrington may well have been worn by the Prophet Francis himself.

The significance of his descriptions aside, the use of the phrase "dressed-up apes" to describe the Creek and Seminole leaders reveals much about British opinions of their allies. Even Andrew Jackson, the hated enemy of the Red Sticks, did not refer to them in such terms.

While the families – including Milly's – remained behind at Prospect Bluff, some of the Red Stick and Seminole chiefs and warriors accompanied the British aboard ship to Louisiana for the planned attack on New Orleans. They were witnesses to the slaughter inflicted on the British by Andrew Jackson's army at Chalmette on January 8, 1815. They returned to the Apalachicola to tell the story:

...They were beaten in every battle by night and by day. Their large Vessels could not come near the land, they sent their troops in barges who were attacked as they were landing, and at night after landing. He saw the decisive battle on the 8th. The Americans had double ditches which were not discovered til they got up to the first, the first who attempted to storm the works were driven back with great loss. A second attempt was made, which met a similar fate, when the Commander in Chief went forward with his best troops, who met with a greater loss, he was killed and the next in command. The ground appeared to him covered with dead wounded and the British had many wounded who retreated in action or were carried off.[11]

The news was disappointing and disillusioning to warriors and their families alike, but Colonel Nicolls worked to motivate them and continued to prepare his command for the planned invasion of Georgia. A second fort was built on the east bank of the Apalachicola at what is now Chattahoochee Landing just below the confluence of the Chattahoochee and Flint Rivers. Even as the main army was being devastated by Jackson at the Battle of New Orleans, British officers on the Apalachicola were able to report that by January their force had grown to include 3,551 warriors. These included 1,421 Lower Creeks and Seminoles from towns on the Apalachicola and lower Chattahoochee and Flint Rivers, 800 Red Sticks, 400 warriors from the Chehaw towns on the Flint, 760 Seminoles from Miccasukee and the Suwannee and 180 Africans from east of the Apalachicola. This total did not include the battalion of black Colonial Marines inducted into the British service by Nicolls and Woodbine or the Red Sticks still hiding along the Conecuh and Choctawhatchee Rivers.[12]

More warriors now were ready to take the field than Francis and his followers had commanded at the height of their power during the Creek War. In addition, they were much better equipped. The British had provided them with thousands of muskets and carbines, as well as sabers, powder, shot, gunflints, cartridge boxes and bayonets. They also had received at least rudimentary training in small arms tactics and were supported by both Colonial and Royal Marines. The latter organization had brought ashore a battery of field guns to add additional firepower to the assembled force that numbered well over 4,000 men.

It was not to be. Although British forces came ashore on Cumberland and St. Simons Islands on the Georgia coast and Nicolls dispatched some small raiding and scouting parties into the interior of Georgia, news of the Treaty of Ghent arrived on the Apalachicola even as the British were preparing to battle a force of U.S.-allied Creeks led in person by Colonel Hawkins. Both Francis and McQueen were on hand and in British uniform at the upper fort when news of the treaty arrived. The War of 1812 was over, but they were assured by British officers that the 9th article of the treaty required that the two nations return to the borders they had occupied at the beginning of the conflict. The British believed this meant that the Treaty of Fort Jackson was invalid and that the lands ceded under it would be returned to the Creeks.[13]

A council was convened at the upper fort on March 10, 1815, between Nicolls and 30 Seminole and Red Stick chiefs. Present for the talks were Francis, McQueen, Kenhajo, Hopoithlemico (Homathlemico), Neamathla and others. They drafted and signed an agreement with Nicolls that voided land grants to the Forbes company and requested that the British open trade with them through the Alabama, Apalachicola and St. Mary's Rivers. The chiefs also swore allegiance to King George III and agreed that future land sales would be subject to British consent. They agreed also to grant land to any British subjects who came and settled among them.[14]

The upper fort was evacuated soon after the conference and preparations began for a British departure from the post at Prospect Bluff. The chiefs who met in council at the upper fort had nominated Francis to go back to England with Colonel Nicolls to represent them to the Prince Regent. He agreed to go and it was probably at this time that he relocated his family from the bluff to the Wakulla River.

The new town site was chosen for the security it offered as well as its proximity to the Spanish post of San Marcos de Apalache (Fort St. Marks). Located on the east bank of the Wakulla River three miles above the fort, it stood in a river margin of rich land facing the crystal clear stream at today's Hyde Park community which is just a few miles below the source of the river at spectacular Wakulla Springs. It was and still is a place of remarkable beauty.

Milly was around 12 years old when her family relocated to its new home on the banks of the Wakulla. Although houses needed to be built and fields cleared, it seemed that the specter of war had disappeared. Her father and her young brother Earle left with Colonel Nicolls in May 1815, but Milly and the rest of the family was now in a place of security where they could obtain food and begin to settle down and return to life as normal.

---

[1] Dale Cox, "The Battle of Fort Bowyer," online article at www.ExploreSouthernHistory.com, 2012.

[2] Sugden, p. 296.

[3] David Crockett, *A Narrative of the Life of David Crockett, of the State of Tennessee*.

[4] *Ibid.*

[5] Capt. Robert Henry to Admiral Alexander Cochrane, November 22, 1814, CP, 2328, p. 126.

[6] *Ibid.*

[7] Pintado map of the Apalachicola.

[8] *Ibid.*

[9] Edward Codrington, *Memoir of the life of Admiral Sir Edward Codrington*, p. 239.

[10] *Ibid.*

[11] Description of the Battle of New Orleans by an anonymous Red Stick chief as written by Col. Benjamin Hawkins to Gov. Peter Early, February 12, 1815, Telamon Cuyler Collection, UGA, Box 76, Folder 25, Document 20.

[12] Sugden, p. 298.
[13] Col. Benjamin Hawkins to Gov. Peter Early, February 26, 1815, Telamon Cuyler Collection, UGA, Box 76, Folder 25, Document 23.
[14] Indian Agreement, WO/1/143/147-150.

Photographs

Site of the citadel of the British Post on the Apalachicola

Water Battery of the British Post on the Apalachicola

General Sir Edward Nicolls (late in life)
Courtesy of Nigel Moss, descendent of General Nicolls.

Andrew Jackson, Major General & President (late in life)

Benjamin Hawkins, U.S. Agent for Indian Affairs

Fort Jackson near Wetumpka, Alabama (scene of treaty signing)

Sam and Ben Perryman, Creek warriors

Bataria de San Antonio (left) at Pensacola Bay, occupied by British in 1814

Pensacola Bay

Photographs

Julee's Cottage, home of free African American free African American woman at Pensacola Historic Village, was standing when Red Sticks reached Pensacola.

Lavalle House at Historic Pensacola Village, stood when Red Sticks reached Pensacola

Chapter Six

The First Seminole War

LIFE ON THE WAKULLA MUST HAVE BEEN A RELIEF to Milly, her mother and sister after the terror and tragedies they had experienced during the Creek War and their flight from Alabama. The beautiful river was ideal for swimming and play and supplies were plentiful and available from the nearby Seminole towns of Tallahassee Talofa and Miccosukee. Trade goods could be obtained from the Spanish fort. Slowly but surely the family recovered from its great losses. A new home was built and Milly and her sister played along the river. The sound of laughter returned to their town.

Across the Atlantic, the Prophet stayed with Colonel Nicolls at his home of Durham Lodge near Eltham, Kent. He tried to secure a meeting for Francis with Earl Bathurst, but received little in the way of a response. The Earl did order that Francis be presented with a pair of custom pistols, but expressed no interest in meeting with him. Nicolls pleaded the case of his guest, pointing out to British leaders that the Prophet had come from thousands of miles away as a representative of Indians who had been firm allies of the British during the recently closed war. He explained in writing that the Prophet and the members of his delegation needed winter clothing and also told Bathurst that a request had been made for Earle to be educated in England. British high command, however, remained silent to the colonel's pleas.[1]

When Nicolls left the Apalachicola, he had turned the Prospect Bluff fort over to his Indian and black allies, along with its heavy guns and a massive stockpile of ammunition, small arms and accoutrements. With the exception of a handful of Choctaws, the warriors soon returned to their villages, leaving the fort under the command of Garcon, the sergeant major, who promised to defend it. The total population at the bluff dwindled to around 320 men, women and children. With the artillery, however, there were enough men to wage a strong defense should they be attacked by an enemy. Red Stick and Seminole chiefs and warriors came and went from time to time to secure arms or to replenish their ammunition, but the fort evolved into a settlement occupied almost exclusively by free blacks. Fields were cleared for miles above the fort and the inhabitants settled into new lives in the presumed security of Spanish Florida.

On July 27, 1816, however, Milly and her friends on the Wakulla heard a distinct roar and felt the ground shake beneath their feet. Her head likely was filled with memories of the New Madrid earthquakes she had experienced in 1811-1812, but this time the explanation was not natural phenomena. U.S. forces had attacked the fort at Prospect Bluff – a placed they called the Negro Fort – and blown it to bits. A red hot cannonball fired from a U.S. Navy gunboat sailed through the entrance to the gunpowder magazine and the fort exploded in a blast that could be felt as far away as Pensacola.

Of the 320 men, women and children in the fort, 270 were killed in an instant. American officers described how pieces of their bodies were thrown for great distances, in some cases even landing in the tops of the tall longleaf pines that surrounded the destroyed fort. Most of the 50 survivors were seriously wounded and many died in the hours and days after the blast. The shot that hit the magazine of the Fort on the Apalachicola was the deadliest cannon shot in American history. Milly Francis and the other residents of her village on the Wakulla were close enough to feel the blast.

Hundreds of warriors from throughout the region had started out to oppose the Americans as soon as word spread that an attack against the depot was in the making. Red Sticks from the towns of Francis and McQueen were likely among them and word reached Colonel Duncan L. Clinch that he would have to fight his way back upriver. When the Americans reached the scene of the anticipated battle, however, the Red Stick and Seminole force had disappeared. The explosion so stunned the warriors that they withdrew from the confrontation until they could better determine what had happened.

Milly and the other residents of the Prophet's town on the Wakulla must have worried if additional attacks were coming, but a shaky peace returned to North Florida following the destruction of the Fort on the Apalachicola. The chiefs and warriors were outraged over the attack and by the confiscation of their weapons and ammunition from the surviving magazines. The Americans kept the cannon for themselves, but the small arms and powder by pre-arrangement was given to William McIntosh and his U.S.-allied Creek warriors. Since McIntosh was a mortal enemy of Francis and McQueen, the delivery to him of the stockpile left behind for their use by Colonel Nicolls was a severe blow.

Josiah Francis was still in England when the attack took place and did not learn of the disaster until his return to the Caribbean that winter. Although he received a number of personal gifts for himself and his family, he began his return trip home in December without the British support he had hoped to secure. At New Providence in the Bahamas he met with Captain Woodbine and Governor Cameron, both of whom were more optimistic about the prospects of supplying the Indians.

Woodbine in particular sought to secure an alliance with the Prophet. No longer in the British military, he had converted his career to one of an adventurer and filibusterer. Having learned firsthand during the War of 1812 that the Spanish forces holding Florida were remarkably weak, Woodbine adopted the old dream of William Augustus Bowles who during the late 18th century had tried to seize control of the colony by declaring the independence of an Indian nation that he called the "State of Muskogee." Now, with help from former British lieutenant Robert Ambrister, Woodbine organized an effort to take Florida from Spain. Probably to the detriment of his proposed alliance with the Red Sticks and Seminoles, however, he also helped himself to some of the gifts that had been given to the Prophet Francis.

Francis had reached New Providence just as the trader Alexander Arbuthnot was about to leave on a journey to open trade with the Seminoles and Red Sticks. Arranging transport on Arbuthnot's schooner, the *Chance*, the Prophet returned to Florida, reaching his village on the Wakulla River in March or April of 1817.

His return after a two-year absence must have been cause for great celebration with his family and followers. Earle had been left behind in England where Colonel Nicolls promised to see to his education, but Milly and her older sister were on the Wakulla and both had grown into young women during their father's absence. Milly was now 14 and her sister was a year or two older. They loved their father deeply and had no way of knowing that their reunion with him marked the beginning of the final year of his life.

Francis returned to Florida just as tension was again surging in the borderlands. Following the evacuation of Fort Scott on the lower Flint River by Colonel Clinch and the 4th U.S. Infantry in December 1816, Red Stick warriors went to the post and burned it to the ground. News of this incident spread up through channels and Major General Edmund P. Gaines ordered two companies from the 4th Battalion, U.S. Artillery, down from Charleston to serve as "red-legged infantry" and return the fort to a defensible condition. Captain Samuel Donoho and his men reached Fort Scott in June 1817 and started the slow and laborious process of rebuilding the buildings and defenses. They were reinforced in July by Brevet Major David E. Twiggs and his company from the 7th U.S. Infantry.

Twiggs had barely assume command at Fort Scott when he was confronted by the Fowltown chief who warned him not to cross to or cut wood from the opposite bank of the Flint River. Neamathla (Eneah Emathla) had converted to the Prophet's cause in 1813. He and his warriors started out to join Francis on the Alabama River, but were intercepted and defeated by William McIntosh and the Coweta warriors from Coweta at the Battle of Uchee Creek in what is now Russell County, Alabama. Pursued by the U.S.-allied Creeks, Neamathla fell back to his town near present-day Leesburg, Georgia, and withdrew his people down the Flint to a new location about three miles south of today's city of Bainbridge.

The chief had not been a party to the Treaty of Fort Jackson, which ceded away all of Southwest Georgia to the Americans, and did not consider himself bound by it. He informed Major Twiggs that the land south of the Flint was his and that he was "directed by the Powers Above to defend it" and would do so. The Americans later corrupted what Neamathla had said, changing it to read that he claimed to be "directed by the Powers Above AND BELOW." The implication of this change was clear - Neamathla was in league with the Devil.

Even as the confrontation grew between Neamathla and the U.S. Army, Josiah Francis began to preach caution. He had witnessed such death and destruction during the Creek War and then had seen his people abandoned by their supposed British allies:

...The notorious Francis is crestfallen and begins to think with us that the Indians should learn to behave themselves, altho' the American Commandant at

the Forks had a hearing with some of the disaffected chiefs, the events did not prove satisfactory to either parties; I now almost believe to a certainty they must be scourged into obedience.[2]

The Prophet's conversion to the cause of peace aside, the Secretary of War ordered General Gaines to remove Neamathla and his followers from lands ceded to the United States by the Treaty of Fort Jackson. The full strength of the First Brigade was ordered to Fort Scott from Fort Montgomery and Camp Montpelier in Alabama and the troops began the long overland march, cutting a new road to Fort Gaines on the Chattahoochee River and from there down to Fort Scott. As they marched by land, Major Peter Muhlenburg brought their artillery, munitions, spare uniforms and other supplies from Mobile to the Apalachicola River by way of the Gulf of Mexico. He was still on the lower river when Lieutenant Richard W. Scott was ordered downstream with a detachment of 40 men to assist the vessels in coming up to the fort.

As the water operations were underway, the main body of the First Brigade reached Fort Scott on November 19, 1817. General Gaines had preceded the troops to the fort and immediately ordered Major Twiggs to take 250 men to Fowltown and bring back Neamathla and his leading men. They were to avoid conflict if possible, but given the discretion to defend themselves if necessary. Twiggs marched out on November 20th and reached Fowltown before dawn the next morning.

The American plan was to quietly surround the town in the dark so that its inhabitants could be captured without gunfire. As the troops moved into position, Neamathla and his warriors discovered their presence and opened fire. The troops responded with a volley from their muskets, killing several of the town's inhabitants, including a woman. Although the chief and most of his people, escaped into the surrounding swamp, the first shots of the Seminole Wars had been fired.

Aside from taking a few head of cattle, the troops were restrained from looting Fowltown. The various houses and buildings were examined. In the home of Neamathla was found a red British uniform coat and a letter from a British officer testifying that the chief had always been a loyal friend. His mission unsuccessful, Twiggs returned to Fort Scott and informed General Gaines of what had taken place. Short of supplies and learning from Twiggs of the presence of a large amount of corn in the Indian corncribs, the general ordered a second strike against Fowltown.

This mission was led by Lieutenant Colonel Matthew Arbuckle and involved 300 men from the 4th and 7th U.S. Infantry Regiments. Reaching Fowltown on November 23, 1817, they found the village abandoned and began to fill their wagons with corn from the Indian storehouses. Neamathla suddenly emerged from the surrounding swamp with 60 warriors and with a war cry opened fire on the American soldiers. The U.S. troops returned fire and the Battle of Fowltown raged for about 20 minutes until the Creeks, running low on ammunition, abandoned the fight and fell back into the swamp. Private Aaron Hughes, a fifer in the 7th U.S. Infantry, was killed. He was the first American soldier to die in the Seminole Wars, a series of conflicts that continued until the eve of the Civil War four decades later.

Alarmed by the ferocity of the attack, Arbuckle pulled his men back to the river crossing at present-day Bainbridge and threw up a blockhouse that he named Fort Hughes. The unfortunate fifer was buried on the grounds and Captain John McIntosh was left with 40 men to hold the new outpost. The rest of the soldiers returned to Fort Scott, having consumed all of the captured supplies by the time they arrived.

News of the fighting electrified the Seminole, Red Stick and African towns along the border. Neamathla logically believed that he and his people had been attacked and called for reinforcements. General Gaines, meanwhile, did not consider his raids on Fowltown to have been provocations and instead blamed the warriors of the village for opening the war by firing on his troops instead of allowing themselves to be captured. Aware that U.S. supply vessels were still trying to make their way up the Apalachicola River to Fort Scott, thousands of warriors began to move in that direction. Probably due to his Creek War experience, the chiefs selected the Prophet Francis to lead the operation.

As he assembled his main force at a sharp bend of the river between the Ocheesee town and the high bluffs of today's Torreya State Park, Francis dispatched a smaller force of several hundred warriors to the forks of the Chattahoochee and Flint Rivers. Led by the old Red Stick chief Homathlimico, they attacked the vessel of Lieutenant Richard W. Scott as it made its way back up to Fort Scott with supplies and 20 sick men from Muhlenburg's command. Also on board were 7 women and 4 children, family members of soldiers at the fort. The detachment was guarded by 20 armed soldiers.

The attack ended in bloody massacre. Only 7 people from Scott's party survived. The lieutenant, 34 men, 6 women and 4 children were killed. The children were killed by warriors who picked them up by the ankles and dashed their heads against the sides of the boat. The dead were scalped and otherwise mutilated and Lieutenant Scott was killed by having lightwood splinters driven into his body and then set afire. According to Elizabeth Stewart, the only female survivor, he begged her to take a hatchet from one of the warriors and kill him, but she would not.[3]

The six soldiers who escaped did so by leaping from the boat and swimming across the river to the opposite bank. Five of them were wounded by Red Stick gunfire.. The people of Tomatly, a nearby town that had not joined the war effort, took care of them and helped them get to Fort Scott where they arrived on December 2, 1817. The news of the Scott Massacre stunned the entire post and Gaines immediately wrote to Secretary of War John C. Calhoun and Major General Andrew Jackson to inform them of the attack. The details of his report were published in newspapers along the route as it made its way north to Washington, D.C. An infuriated President James Monroe directed that General Jackson be ordered to the frontier and that the Seminoles and Red Sticks be punished without regard to whether they were in the United States or across the border in Spanish Florida.[4]

The war was now irreversible. War parties surrounded both Fort Scott and Fort Hughes, sniping at any person who showed his or her head in the open. A party lead by the Fowltown chief Chenubby struck at Spanish Bluffs (present-day Bristol, Florida) where William Hambly owned a farm. He and his fellow Forbes & Company employee Edmund Doyle were taken prisoner and carried away first to Miccosukee and then on to Boleck's town on the Suwannee River. William Perryman, the chief from the lower Chattahoochee River who had fought on the side of the British during the American Revolution and War of 1812, realized the futility of opposing the Americans and at their request had gone down to protect Hambly and Doyle. He was killed in the attack on Hambly's plantation and his surviving warriors forced to join the war party.

The Prophet Francis in person led the main force against Major Muhlenburg and the supply flotilla on December 15, 1817. The large sailing vessels were trying to navigate the sharp bend between Ocheesee Bluff in what is now Calhoun County and Rock Bluff at today's Torreya State Park when hundreds of warriors attacked from both sides of the river. More than one dozen soldiers fell killed or wounded and the fire poured into the boats was so severe that the sailors could not show themselves to navigate. Forced to drop anchor at midstream, the men on the vessels were exposed to fire day and night.

The Battle of Ocheesee continued for nearly one week and warriors kept up sporadic fire on the American vessels even after additional troops came down from Fort Scott to help them break free. Other war parties spread up and down the Apalachicola River to skirmish with a detachment of soldiers on its way downstream in a boat to look for any signs of provision vessels then expected at the bay.

The Prophet's plan for the execution of the war was working. Fort Hughes was evacuated and Fort Scott had been cut off and its garrison placed at risk of starvation. The Apalachicola River was blocked and small war parties ranged deep into Georgia to strike isolated homes and unwary travelers.

---

[1] Sugden, p. 308.

[2] Edmund Doyle to John Innerarity, July 11, 1817, *Florida Historical Quarterly*, Volume 18, Issue 02, October 1939, p. 136.

[3] J.B. Rodgers, Eyewitness Account of the First Seminole War as quoted by James Parton, *Life of Andrew Jackson*, Volume 2, Houghton, Mifflen and Company, 1888, p. 456.

[4] For a detailed account of the massacre and its results, please see Dale Cox, *The Scott Massacre of 1817*.

Chapter Seven

Milly Francis & Robert Ambrister

EVEN AS TENSIONS GREW ALONG THE BORDER, Milly Francis became involved in one of the most remarkable episodes of her life. Her father had returned from England bearing gifts for his family, among them beautiful dresses for his daughters and wife. The Prophet's commitment to traditional ways had been altered by the destruction of his movement in Alabama and his subsequent sojourn across the Atlantic at the home of Colonel Nicolls.

Now a girl of 14, Milly was a beautiful young woman, but it had been so long since she had dressed in European style clothing that she was unable to decide how various parts of her new wardrobe should be worn. For help she went to the only person who might know, the newly arrived former lieutenant Robert Ambrister. He had been part of Colonel Nicolls force on the Apalachicola River three years previous and he and Milly were at least acquainted. She had blossomed into a beautiful young woman over the intervening years and now captivated Ambrister's interest.

The story of the friendship that grew between Milly Francis and Robert Ambrister is known from only one source, Dr. J.B. Rodgers of Tennessee. A surgeon with Jackson's army, he treated sick and wounded soldiers at Fort St. Marks after it was taken by the Americans in April 1818. There he became acquainted with both Ambrister and Milly. While he spoke to her only on occasion, Rodgers did have several long conversations with Ambrister, who was then being held as a prisoner in the bombproof of the old Spanish fort.[1]

According to Dr. Rodgers, Milly had been "extremely, though chastely, intimate with Ambrister." The former British officer told the surgeon that he had been a guest in the home of the Prophet Francis for a considerable time:

...There Ambrister said he had found a most interesting daughter of the prophet's, a most exquisitely handsome girl of about seventeen summers, modest and coy, not bashful but natively diffident. When the father unpacked the presents for Milly and gave them to her, she was at some loss to know how to use them. The dresses were not such fits as could have been made in Paris or London. In the last extremity Milly applied to Ambrister for help, and, to his utter astonishment, he was quite as much at a loss as the girl.[2]

It took the two considerable concentration and trial to decide on the proper way for Milly to wear and alter her new clothes, but finally they succeeded and "Milly lost the appearance of a 'maid of the forest'."[3]

Ambrister bonded with the Prophet and his family, remaining with them for some time in their town on the banks of the Wakulla River. As he became familiar and was accepted in the home – at least according to the story as told by Ambrister to Dr. Rodgers – Josiah Francis suggested to the adventurer that he would not be opposed to him taking Milly as his wife:

[I]t was not long before he became a decided favorite with the family and town. Francis gave intimation that he should be pleased to give his daughter in marriage to Ambrister with three hundred negroes, which Ambrister knew he dared not, at the peril of his high position, refuse to treat with becoming consideration and respect.[4]

In other words, the visiting Englishman could not afford to insult the Prophet Francis if he hoped to carry out his part in bringing Woodbine's plans for the conquest of Florida to fruition.

He and Milly entered into a courtship of sorts. She accompanied him on walks along the banks of the pristine river and sometimes rode on horseback alongside him to visit the daughters of the Spanish commandant at San Marcos de

Apalache (Fort St. Marks). They helped her better fit her dresses and she appears to have been constant friends with them:

...She was most beautiful, he said; he loved the girl for her virtue and modesty. She could talk enough English to make herself understood, and she understood the Spanish and Indian. Ambrister, in all his visits to the young ladies in the fort, was accompanied by Malee (i.e. Milly) as his interpreter, and she often played off her little pranks on him, telling the young ladies at one time that they were married, at another that he was in love with her, but she had discarded him, and like pranks.[5]

Dr. Rodgers, as noted in the description just quoted, was the source of the name Malee or Princess Malee, which is often used to identify Milly Francis. He indicated in his account that he thought the name Milly was a corruption and that "the name in Indian is Malee." Why he thought this is not clear. Throughout her entire life, Milly is never known to have used the name "Malee." On the Creek Census of 1832, on the emigration rolls when she was sent west on the Trail of Tears and in documents referring to her during her years in the Muskogee (Creek) Nation in Oklahoma, she universally identified herself as "Milly."

When a larger view is taken of the Prophet's family, it appears likely that "Milly" is correct. Josiah Francis and his wife, Polly, both had and used Anglicized names. Their three known children also were given Anglicized names: Polly, Milly and Earle. While Milly may have had a name in the Alabama language, the identified herself using her English name throughout her life, just as did the other members of the Francis family.

One of Ambrister's most intriguing discoveries about Milly was that she possessed remarkable riding skills, as one might expect for a young woman raised in the Creek Nation:

Among the presents was a large velvet riding hat, with feathers, fine bridle and saddle, too large for a pony, and but for her admirable skill in equestrianism would often have brought her down, but with the aid of which she often outrode him, even when he was mounted on a black pony whose spirit could only at times be conquered by the application of the Spanish curb and rowel...Malee [sic.]could stand on the ground and bound into the saddle and ride off, with her black, flowing hair and feathers streaming in the wind, before he could climb on his gray headed black.[6]

Milly's favorite gait, according to Ambrister, was a gallop and he was hard pressed to keep up with her on horseback.

Despite the intimate friendship – or courtship – that developed between the two, Ambrister swore to Dr. Rodgers that their relationship never became physical. "Ambrister declared," he wrote, "that, except at the time he pinned Malee's [*sic.*] dress, he was never permitted to put his hands on her."

Ambrister's story, as told to Dr. Rodgers, is remarkable in that it sheds much light on Milly Francis as a person. She was a virtuous young woman, but not just in affairs of the heart. The story of her friendship with Robert Ambrister is filled with details about her sense of humor, athleticism and equestrian skills. Her hair was long and black and she was conscious of her appearance, so much so that even after receiving help with her dresses from Ambrister, she went straight to the Spanish girls at the fort for guidance and assistance. The description of her leaping from the ground directly into her saddle demonstrates a remarkable state of physical conditioning. It is a feat rarely seen today.

Unfortunately, the idyllic moments of Milly's life were few and far between. Tragedy stalked her for all of the years she spent on the earth and it was not far removed during the days that she and Ambrister rode and flirted on the banks of Florida's Wakulla River.

---

[1] James Parton, *Life of Andrew Jackson*, Volume 2, Houghton, Mifflin and Company, 1888, pp. 480-481.
[2] *Ibid.*, p. 481.
[3] *Ibid.*
[4] *Ibid.*
[5] *Ibid.*
[6] *Ibid.*, p. 482.

Brigadier General David E. Twiggs, who as a brevet major led the first U.S. attack on Fowltown.

Major General Edmund P. Gaines. He ordered the attacks on Fowltown, sparking the First Seminole war.

Neamathla (Eneah Emathla). He battled U.S. expansion in the First Seminole War and Creek War of 1836.

Brigadier General William McIntosh. He led U.S. allied Creek troops in the first Creek and Seminole wars.

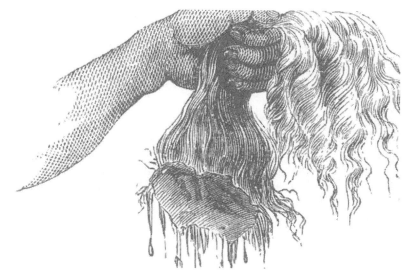

19th Century drawing of a human scalp

19th Century artist's impression of the Scott Massacre

Wakulla River at the site of the Prophet's town

Edward Ball Wakulla Springs State Park

Photographs

Apalachee Bay

Ruins of Spanish fort at San Marcos de Apalache Historic State Park

Chapter Eight

The Creek Pocahontas

THE WINTER OF 1817-1818 WAS ONE OF THE COLDEST ON RECORD in North America. Part of what is now called the "Little Ice Age," it was a time of remarkable climate change throughout the world. Caused by the inconceivable amount of ash poured into the atmosphere by a massive volcanic explosion in the Pacific Ocean, the sudden shift in climate caused crop failures and starvation around the world.

The previous year, 1816, is remembered still today as the "Year Without a Summer." Strange weather destroyed the corn crops in New England and the grain crops in Europe. Hundreds of thousands of people died and food riots shattered the peace even of Switzerland. In North America, the light of day glowed in a strange orange or golden color and unseasonable and severe cold persisted far longer into the growing season than anyone could remember. The unusual weather patterns continued through the winter of 1818.

Trudging through ice and snow that persisted deep into Southwest Georgia, Andrew Jackson and his army reached Fort Scott on March 9, 1818. With crop failures causing problems across the country, the military contractors had been unable to deliver required supplies to the fort by the time of Jackson's arrival. As he assumed command of the stockade on the morning of March 10th, he found himself at the head of an army of more than 2,000 men with nothing more in the way of supplies than about one pint of corn per man and 1,100 head of hogs.[1]

Believing that supply vessels were either at Apalachicola Bay or on their way up the river, Jackson ordered the hogs slaughtered and issued all of his remaining provisions to his men. He then crossed the Flint River from Fort Scott and on March 11, 1818, marched into Spanish Florida. It was the general's second invasion of a foreign country in less than four years.

The army pushed down the high bluffs that dominate the east side of the Apalachicola River, passing through what is now Gadsden County to Alum Bluff in Liberty County. Jackson's scouts spotted the desperately needed supply vessels making their way up the river, so the army halted and the men were given a day of rest atop the beautiful heights. The soldiers were given an extra day's ration to stimulate their morale after the hunger they had suffered over the preceding weeks.[2]

The Americans continued down the east side of the Apalachicola and reached Prospect Bluff on March 16, 1818. The old British water battery was still intact, as were the outer ditches and breastworks, but the central citadel of the fort was just a crater surrounded by mounds of earth. The effects of the explosion of the magazine during the attack of July 27, 1816, could be seen everywhere:

...We found some of their arms and cannon ball lying in the mud. The guns, although they had been exposed to the weather for four years [sic. two years], when put in the fire to burn the rust off, would fire. Here we erected a new fort upon the ruins of the old one and called it Fort Gadsden.[3]

It took the army eight days to build the new much more compact fort. Jackson's engineer, Lieutenant James Gadsden, designed and supervised the construction of the citadel. The former British water battery was used to form the river front of the fort with a rectangular bastioned affair being added onto it. The earthworks of both the British battery and the American fort are well-preserved today at Fort Gadsden Historic Site in the Apalachicola National Forest. The new fort was much smaller than the War of 1812 complex and much of the interior of the earlier work was used as its field of fire. Jackson was so pleased with the project that he named the new post in Lieutenant Gadsden's honor.

During the time that the soldiers were engaged in building Fort Gadsden, many of the men found themselves with idle time on their hands. Nine hundred of the men forming Jackson's army were newly enlisted Georgia militiamen and discipline was not their strong suit. Among them was a young solder named Duncan McCrimmon and – at least according to the story as told in 1818 – the lure of finding a good fishing hole along the banks of the river or one of its tributary creeks was too strong for him to deny.

A resident of the Milledgeville area, McCrimmon was a member of Captain Joseph Watters' company of the 1st Georgia Militia Regiment, commanded by Brigadier General Thomas Glascock. His unit had been formed in January by order of Governor William Rabun in response to a call for Georgia to provide additional troops to support the U.S. Army during the coming campaign. The men accompanied Jackson on his way south to Fort Scott where they were joined by the regular soldiers of the 4th and 7th U.S. Infantry Regiments.

Although his name is usually spelled "McKrimmon" by modern writers, he spelled it "McCrimmon" as do his living descendants. As seems to be the case with Milly Francis – who often is referred to as "Princess Malee" – Duncan McCrimmon has been remembered through the use of an incorrect name.

Why McCrimmon would drift so far away from Fort Gadsden and become lost in the woods is questionable, especially with the sure knowledge that Red Stick and Seminole scouts were in the vicinity watching the activities of the Americans. Trying to make his way back to the fort from his day of fishing, he found himself turned around and confused. He wound up wandering in the wilderness of today's Apalachicola National Forest for several days, completely lost and unable to find his way.[4]

While in this condition, he stumbled across two warriors from the Prophet's Town. They had been sent to gather intelligence on the movements of Jackson's army and quickly took the hapless militiaman as their captive:

After wandering about in various directions, he was espied and captured by a party of hostile Indians, headed by the well known prophet Francis – who had an elegant uniform, a fine brace of pistols, and a British commission of brigadier general which he exultingly shewed to the prisoner. Having obtained the satisfaction they wanted respecting the strength and position of the American army, they began to prepare for the intended sacrifice.[5]

There are many versions of what happened next, but the earliest are those that appeared in the Milledgeville newspapers in November 1818. They appear to have been based on an account provided to the editors by Lieutenant Colonel Matthew Arbuckle, then commanding at Fort Gadsden. A man who enjoyed writing, Arbuckle was a regular correspondent of the Milledgeville papers. The editors may have benefited as well from conversations with McCrimmon himself, who by that time had returned back home in Georgia.

As the story was told at the time, the warriors were on the verge of executing McCrimmon when a Pocahontas-like story unfolded:

M'Krimmon was planted at a stake, and the ruthless savages having shaved his head, and reduced his body to a state of nudity, formed themselves in a circle and danced several hours, yelling all the while most horribly. The youngest daughter of the prophet, (who is about 15 years of age and represented by officers of the army we have conversed with to be a woman very superior to her associates) was sad and silent the whole time – she participated not in the general joy, but was evidently, even to the affrighted prisoner, much pained at the savage scene she was compelled to witness.[6]

The "youngest daughter of the Prophet," of course, was Milly Francis. She had been playing on the banks of the Wakulla River with her sister when they heard the war whoop of warriors. Going into the village to investigate, they found that some of the men had brought in a white prisoner:

When the fatal tomahawk was raised to terminate forever the mortal existence of the unfortunate M'Krimmon, at that critical, that awful moment, Milly Francis, like an angel of mercy, placed herself between it and death, resolutely bidding the astonished executioner if he thirsted for human blood, to shed her's; being determined, she said, not to survive the prisoner's death. A momentary pause was produced by this unexpected occurrence, and she took advantage of the circumstance to implore the pity of her ferocious father – who finally yielded to her wishes with the intention, however, it is believed, of murdering them both, if he could not sell M'Krimmon to the Spaniards, which was luckily effected a few days after at St. Marks, for seven gallons and a half of rum.[7]

Despite the editor's fantastic claim, there is no evidence of any kind that Josiah Francis planned to murder his daughter along with McCrimmon at some later time. Like most fathers, he loved his children and wanted only the best for them. The Prophet had seen to the education of his young son, Earle, before leaving England and he had returned to Florida with extravagant gifts for his daughters. Throughout the Creek War and War of 1812, he had seen to the safety of his family and – American opinions of him aside – there is no reason to believe he was anything other than a devoted father and husband.

McCrimmon was taken to San Marcos de Apalache (Fort St. Marks) and turned over to the commandant there. Evidence exists that the Spanish officer did in fact ransom the young citizen soldier for a supply of rum. McCrimmon joined two other prisoners – William Hambly and Edmund Doyle – who already were under the care and protection of the Spanish.

The three prisoners were allowed freedom within the perimeters of the post but the commandant cautioned them not to stray past those lines lest they be recaptured by the Red Sticks.

The remarkable story of the "new Pocahontas" fascinated readers across the country and newspapers as far away as Maine reprinted the articles originating from Milledgeville. Updates on her condition and whereabouts were published throughout the years 1818 and 1819 by newspapers all over the United States. Americans have always loved heroes, and Milly Francis became the heroine of her day.

Milly told the story many times over the years that followed to dozens of interested people, but her actual words were not recorded until more than two decades later when Lieutenant Colonel Ethan Allen Hitchcock found her living in the Creek Nation of present-day Oklahoma. Sent west to investigate conditions among the tribes and to get to investigate reports of frauds committed on the Indians, Hitchcock was at Fort Gibson in the Cherokee Nation when he learned that the famed Creek Pocahontas lived nearby.

On the afternoon of January 27, 1842, Colonel Hitchcock rode from Fort Gibson to the nearby trading post of Seaborn Hill. In his conversation with Mr. Hill, Hitchcock learned that Milly Francis lived only one mile away. Fascinated, he sent a messenger to see if she would consent to come and visit him. She soon appeared with her youngest son, who was then around 14 years of age:

...I spoke of the story of her having saved the life of a white man and she at once told me the whole story. During the war (1817-18) it was "given out" that if any Indian caught a white man that he had the life of the white man in his power, (no chief even could save him). Milly heard a war whoop and going to the place

that two Indians had a young white man tied and perfectly naked; other Indians came around and Milly described the white man doubling himself to screen himself from the gaze of those that were looking at him and at the same time looking anxiously around as if to ask if there was no one to speak for him and save his life.[8]

Milly told Hitchcock that the warriors were not preparing to burn McCrimmon at the stake, as most reports indicated at the time, but instead were about to shoot him. She recalled that she was but "a little girl" at the time and that she felt great sadness for him:

Seeing the young man and thinking it a "pity" he should be killed she went to her father and urged that it was a pity, etc. The father said, go to the men who have the right over the young man's life. She went to them and began to plead. One of them said he should die for that, he had had two sisters killed. She told him that to kill a white man would not bring back his sisters and that he was but a boy and had not the "head" of a man to guide him – (the meaning of this was that he was not old enough to have engaged in the war upon his own judgment). Milly prevailed on the condition that the lad should have his head shaved and live with the Indians.[9]

Milly's story differed from the original newspaper accounts in that she said McCrimmon's head was shaved after he agreed to the terms she presented him, not before as part of the execution ritual. This is logical since Creek warriors of the time often shaved all of their heads except for the scalp locks down the top and strips across the front. If McCrimmon had agreed to live as one of them, then they probably would have shaved his head in the same way as their own. When Milly explained the terms to him, she recalled that he said, "Yes, Yes, cut it all off if you choose!" They then shaved his head "except for the scalp lock" and he was turned loose and dressed.[10]

Searching her memory, Milly verified to Major Hitchcock that McCrimmon had been sold to the Spanish for a barrel of whiskey. The Prophet's teachings against alcohol had gone by the wayside with the destruction of his movement during the Creek War of 1813-1814. The sale or ransoming of Duncan McCrimmon to the Spanish – even though he had agreed to become a member of the village – probably was done as a way to protect him from harm. Many of the followers of the Prophet Francis had lost wives, sons and daughters during the

Creek War and flight from Alabama. Resentment to one of their enemies living among them must have been strong.

Even as Milly Francis carried out her act of mercy to Duncan McCrimmon, Andrew Jackson and the American army were on the move. With additional supplies having reached Fort Gadsden on March 24, 1818, along with intelligence via Captain Richard Keith Call that Red Sticks had been to Pensacola to demand arms and ammunition from the Spanish, as well as possession of the fort at San Marcos de Apalache, the general quickly put the next phase of his campaign into action.

Planning to swing north and east around the vast Tate's Hell Swamp of today's Apalachicola National Forest, Jackson requested that Captain Isaac McKeever of the U.S. Navy take the USS *Thomas Shields* out of Apalachicola Bay and around to St. Marks:

...It is reported to me that Francis, or Hillis Hago, and Peter McQueen, prophets, who excited the Red Sticks in their late war against the United States, and are now exciting the Seminoles to similar acts of hostility, are at or in the neighborhood of St. Marks. United with them it is stated that Woodbine, Arbuthnot and other foreigners have assembled a motley crew of brigands – slaves enticed away from their masters, citizens of the United States, or stolen during the late conflict with Great Britain. It is all important that these men should be captured and made examples of, and it is my belief that on the approach of my army they will attempt to escape to some of the sea islands, from whence they may be enabled for a time to continue their excitement, and carry on a predatory war against the United States. You will, therefore, cruise along the coast, eastwardly, and as I advance capture and make prisoners all, or every person, or description of persons, white, red or black, with all their goods, chattels and effects, together with all crafts, vessels or means of transportation by water, which will be held possession of for adjudication.[11]

McKeever was instructed to allow any Spanish vessels to enter the port, but not to permit them to leave until their vessels were inspected to make sure no enemies of the United States were on board. The main army left Fort Gadsden on the same day, Jackson having stated his intent to McKeever to arrive at San Marcos de Apalache in eight days.[12]

War, once again, was coming to Milly Francis.

[1] Dale Cox, *The Scott Massacre of 1817*, 2013, pp. 94.95.

[2] Maj. Gen. Andrew Jackson to John C. Calhoun, Secretary of War, March 25, 1818, *American State Papers*, Military Affairs, Volume 1, pp. 698-699.

[3] John Banks, *Diary of John Banks*, 1936, pp. 9-14.

[4] *Milledgeville Reflector*, November 2, 1818.

[5] *Ibid.*

[6] *Ibid.*

[7] *Ibid.*

[8] Journal of Ethan Allen Hitchcock, January 27, 1842.

[9] *Ibid.*

[10] *Ibid.*

[11] Maj. Gen. Andrew Jackson to Capt. Isaac McKeever, March 26, 1818, from James Parton, *Life of Andrew Jackson*, Volume 2, pp. 447-448.

[12] *Ibid.*

Chapter Nine

The Hanging of the Prophet Francis

BY THE TIME HE ARRIVED OFF THE MOUTH OF THE ST. MARKS RIVER IN APRIL 1818, Lieutenant Isaac McKeever was an American naval hero. As a 23-year-old officer in the U.S. Navy, he commanded one of the five small American gunboats that defied a British flotilla of 42 vessels at the Battle of Lake Borgne in December 1814. The engagement was a preliminary action to the Battle of New Orleans and fired the imagination of the American public when it was learned that the little U.S. Navy squadron had killed or wounded 200 British sailors and marines before it was overwhelmed.[1]

McKeever was wounded in that fight, but returned to duty after the end of the War of 1812 as the captain of the USS *Thomas Shields*, a schooner named for a disabled American officer who had launched a daring raid on the British as they retreated from New Orleans in 1815. The *Shields* escorted the cargo vessels carrying supplies for Jackson's army to the Apalachicola River and then, per his agreement with the general, McKeever took her through St. George Sound to Apalachee Bay. Two supply ships accompanied his movement.

The section of the St. Marks River from the old fort of San Marcos de Apalache down to Apalachee Bay was called the Pinar by the Spanish. It passes through a vast marshland that is now part of the St. Marks National Wildlife

Refuge. The view from the fort looking south across the grass is one of the most beautiful in Florida and is so open that the Spanish lookouts could see the masts of the American vessels as they came into view. Captain Franisco Luengo reported a few weeks later to Governor Don Jose Masot that although he knew the vessels had arrived, "they kept English colors flying until the day before the arrival of the army."[2]

Luengo knew that Jackson's army was on the move, but the intelligence reaching him was contradictory and confusing. He reported to the governor in Pensacola that he could not decide what the Americans planned or were doing and had no reason to believe they were marching on St. Marks. The arrival of ships flying the British flag must have added to his confusion, especially when they made no move to enter the river or to send a small boat up to the fort to announce their presence.

The three prisoners being held in the fort – Edmund Doyle, William Hambly and Duncan McCrimmon - soon approached Captain Luengo to ask permission to row out to the ships. Curiosity probably had the better of the Spanish officer by this point and he granted their request:

McKrimmon, upon seeing a vessel coming into port showing English colors, asked leave of the Spanish commandant to go on board of her, alleging that he feared the Indians might reclaim him and put him to death. He had been consigned to the custody of the Spanish commandant by Francis the prophet, whose town was only three miles distant. He went on board with Hambly and Doyle, who were in the same situation as himself – prisoners subject to Indian caprice. To their equal astonishment and delight, they found that the vessel was American, and that their safety was certain.[3]

McCrimmon and the others gave Lieutenant McKeever fresh intelligence on the situation at San Marcos de Apalache, telling him of the presence there of the Scottish trader Alexander Arbuthnot and of the proximity of the Prophet Francis, Homathlimico and other Red Stick and Seminole leaders. They had been hoping against hope that British vessels would arrive with arms and ammunition to help their war effort and the arrival of the three ships appeared to be the fulfillment of those hopes.

Taking advantage of this information, McKeever increased his display of British colors:

...[T]he temptation was too strong to be longer resisted – Francis or Hellis Hajo, with his right-hand chief, Himollemico, obtained a canoe and set off to the fleet at the mouth of the bay, distant ten miles from the fort. Soon they accomplished their journey, and as soon as they got on board Francis asked:

'What loaded with?'

He was informed, 'guns, powder, lead, and blankets for his red friends the Indians.'[4]

Determined to separate the two leaders from their escort and capture them with as little violence as possible, McKeever invited them down to his cabin to share a drink. Falling completely for the ruse being perpetrated upon them by the lieutenant and his men, Francis and Homathlemico accepted McKeever's invitation:

They manifested ecstatic delight; when the captain invited them to his cabin (taking care to deprive them of all their arms), to take a glass with him. They descended the stairs, the captain following in the rear, with a signal to a few Jack tars to accompany him with ropes. No sooner said than done. Jack made his appearance before the astonished chiefs, who were soon bound and secured beyond the possibility of escape.[5]

McCrimmon, Hambly and Doyle now approached the captive Red Sticks. Duncan drew the immediate attention of the Prophet Francis:

'This is what I get for saving your life.'

'Not so,' said McKrimmon; 'it is to your daughter Milly that I am indebted for my life, and I will do anything I can for your deliverance.'

Mr. Hambly then addressed Himollemico in his language, and told him he was now in the hands of General Jackson, who was hourly expected to invest St. Marks with his army, five thousand strong, and who actually did arrive that very evening as predicted; a thing, however, expected and looked for by the chiefs then in confinement, and who had made a desperate virtue of necessity in coming on board to obtain munitions of war to repel the General, but who had made so sad a mistake.[6]

Not long after the Red Sticks went aboard the *Thomas Shields*, Rodgers and others watched from the deck as another canoe approached. It was paddled by a warrior and carrying a young Creek woman. From a distance, McCrimmon misidentified the woman as Milly Francis. In fact, it was her older sister Polly:

...The sea was increasing and the canoe labored much, until it came near the vessel, when suddenly, either from the force of the sea or some presentiment, the canoe wheeled and put back for the nearest beach, distant a mile. The sentinel on duty hailed without arresting the attention of the occupants of the canoe. He hailed a second, a third time with like results. The captain then ordered the discharge of a cannon to intimidate them, with like result. The captain then ordered a second cannon to be fired, somewhat impatiently. The officer misunderstanding the order, fired a heavy discharge of grape directly at the canoe, the shot falling all around, without the slightest damage to the occupants.[7]

Why the U.S. Navy would see fit to fire on a canoe carrying a young woman has never been explained, but multiple sources confirm that the incident did take place as described by Dr. Rodgers. Realizing the danger, the occupants of the canoe began a desperate attempt to escape:

The captain then manned a light boat, with orders to capture the craft, which sped off at his bidding, and was soon in close pursuit. The canoe, however, approached the land, the water being shallow. Milly [i.e. Polly] bounded from the canoe, and as quick as thought, snatched from the bottom the warrior's rifle, and discharged it at the boat, depositing the ball in the rudder under the arm of the steers-man without further damage. The warrior grasped the empty gun from the hands of Milly [i.e. Polly], and both made safe their retreat to the main land, beyond the reach of the boat's crew, who made it their particular business to be as quick as possible to get beyond the second discharge of the warrior's rifle.[8]

Whether Milly was at the fort watching as the *Thomas Shields* opened fire on the canoe carrying her sister is not known. Dr. Rodgers and others saw her at San Marcos the next day, so it is likely that she did witness the incident or at least that she heard the firing. The cannon fire ended the illusion that the ships at the mouth of the river were British and the Stars and Stripes soon replaced the Union Jack in the wind above their decks.

Andrew Jackson and his army reached the Spanish fort on April 6, 1818. From Fort Gadsden they had marched north and east around Tate's Hell and other swamps of today's Apalachicola National Forest, passing through Franklin,

Liberty and Gadsden Counties. Upon reaching the Ochlockonee River, Jackson crossed his men over into what is now Leon County and the bluff that still bears his name. From there the column pushed forward to Tallahassee Talofa, which was reached on March 31, 1818. The town was abandoned just ahead of the arrival of the troops.

The major Seminole town of Miccosukee was now in range and the next morning Jackson and his army struck. As the soldiers formed a line of battle and advanced on the town, Kenhajo and a party of his warriors took up a position on a peninsula or point that protruded into a pond. They waged a brief but intense fight to allow time for the last of the women and children to escape across Lake Miccosukee to safety in the woods beyond. Once the noncombatants were away, the resistance evaporated and the warriors joined them in flight.

Jackson and his men were stunned by the sheer size of the Miccosukee town. Having been occupied since before the American Revolution, it was a town of long-standing permanence. Hundreds of homes were discovered along with livestock, thousands of bushels of corn, horses and other supplies. The Americans also found a pole decorated with scalps, some of them old but others quite new. The length of the hair told the soldiers that some had come from women and several were recognized as having belonged to the people killed at the Scott Massacre the previous November.

Jackson halted the army in Miccosukee and sent out raiding parties to collect supplies and destroy outlying homes and settlements. The next day, April 2, 1818, he ordered Major General Edmund P. Gaines to take a large force and wade across the shallow lake. Their target was Neamathla, who had relocated his village of Fowltown from Southwest Georgia to the presumed safety of the Miccosukee environs:

...The red pole was again found planted in the square of Fowltown, barbarously decorated with human scalps of both sexes, taken within the last six months from the heads of our unfortunate citizens. General McIntosh, who was with General Gaines, routed a small party of savages near Fowltown, killed one negro, and took three prisoners, on one of whom was found the coat of James Champion, of Captain Cummings's company, (4th regiment of infantry,) who was killed by the Indians on board of one of our boats descending the river to the relief of Major Muhlenburg. This coat, with nearly all Captain Cummings's company's clothing, was lost on board of Lieutenant Scott's boat, when he and his party were massacred, on the 30th of November last.[9]

In Miccosukee itself, the soldiers found a packet belonging to Thomas Leigh, a civilian who had been killed at Cedar Creek near present-day Cordele, Georgia. Still contained in the packet were letters and other documents, among them a report to Brigadier General Thomas Glascock of the Georgia Militia.[10]

The army marched from the Seminole town on the morning of April 5, 1818. The sky behind them was dark with the smoke of more than 300 burning homes as the soldiers began their way south on the trail that led to San Marcos de Apalache. They camped somewhere in between that night and arrived within view of the fort on the evening of the 6th.

San Marcos de Apalache is located on the point of land formed by the confluence of the St. Marks and Wakulla Rivers. A wide expanse of marsh separates the fort from the trees and firmer ground by which the army approached. Hoping to avoid the necessity of having to charge a fortified position across the open wetlands, Jackson sent Lieutenant James Gadsden to the fort to negotiate its surrender. He accused the Spanish at San Marcos of supplying and providing information to the Seminoles and Red Sticks, a charge the Spanish commandant later denied:

...How, then, is it possible to believe that I gave them the aid of which General Jackson complains, or how can such aid be reconciled with the tenor of my letters and the steps I took to liberate Messrs. Edmund Doyle and William Hambly, by which I exposed myself and my garrison to the vengeance of the Indians? Or, lastly, with the fact of my having ransomed, at a most critical moment, an American soldier, whom they declared to me they would otherwise put to death? I leave it to the most impartial to decide, if these be not proofs of the existence, at St. Marks, of a bias in favor of the American interest; and of this, I am persuaded, General Jackson will be convinced on deliberately reflecting on the subject.[11]

The soldier that Luengo mentions having ransomed, of course, was Duncan McCrimmon. He was still aboard the *Thomas Shields*, which remained at the mouth of the river awaiting news from the army that it was safe to move upstream to the fort.

The Spanish commandant objected to Jackson's demand for possession of the fort, but took no steps to prepare for an attack. When the negotiations continued for longer than the general desired, he ordered Major David E. Twiggs to take two companies from the 7th U.S. Infantry Regiment and storm the fort. Twiggs and his men advanced so quickly that they were through the gate and in possession of San Marcos de Apalache before the Spanish soldiers could man the ramparts or fire their cannon. From that morning of April 7, 1818, until the end of its military existence, the Spanish flag never again flew above the old fort.

The fort now in his hands, Jackson sent a boat down the river to inform Lieutenant McKeever that it was safe to bring up his vessels. The *Thomas Shields* led the two cargo vessels up the twisting channel to the fort. Arriving there, Lieutenant McKeever sent the captive Red Sticks ashore and turned them over to the army. Andrew Jackson may have remained at the fort long enough to view his old enemies, but he went back across the marsh to the main camp leaving behind orders that both Francis and Homathlemico should be hanged:

Francis was a handsome man, six feet high; would weigh say some one hundred and fifty pounds; of pleasing manners; conversed well in English and Spanish; humane in his disposition; by no means barbarous – withal a model chief. When he was informed that General Jackson had ordered him to be hanged, he said,

'What! like a dog? Too much. Shoot me, shoot me. I will die willingly if you will let me see General Jackson.'

'He is not here,' said the officer, 'he is out at the encampment with the army.'[12]

The Prophet's request for an interview with Jackson was denied and, so far as is known, the two men never spoke. From the time he had first marched his army into the Creek Nation in 1813, the Prophet Josiah Francis had been the nemesis of Andrew Jackson. The fate of war had put him into the general's hands, but his personal fate had been decided long before. According to the account of Dr. Rodgers, Francis remained Jackson's enemy until the moment of his death:

His hands were then tied behind him, and in the effort to confine him he dropped from the sleeve of his coat a butcher knife, that he said he had intended to kill General Jackson with if he ever laid eyes on him. Francis was dressed with a handsome gray frock coat, a present to him while on his late trip to England. The rest of his dress was Indian. From his appearance, he must have been about forty years of age.[13]

Josiah Francis and Homathlemico were hanged on the level ground in front of the fort. A monument honoring Milly Francis for her role in saving the life of Duncan McCrimmon can be found near the site of the executions today. Dr. Rodgers saw her that day and it is clear that she watched the hangings of her father and Homathlimico. "At times she manifested no concern for the death of her father," Rodgers wrote of her reaction to the horrible scene enacted before her, "and at other times she would be plunged into inconsolable grief."[14]

Unlike Milly, General Jackson did not witness the executions. His biographer John Reid, then a staff officer in the general's command, described his commander's reaction to the news of their deaths:

The sentence dooming them to death, being by its infliction, discharged, the officer to whom the duty had been assigned, approached General Jackson and announced it done: he then inquired the disposition that should be made of their lifeless bodies – "Shall they be thrown overboard?" Jackson, with eyes suffused with tears, looked sternly at him, then said, "Recollect, sir, they are no longer our enemies: justice is satisfied! Let their bodies be decently interred."[15]

Josiah Francis and Homathlimico were buried at Fort St. Marks and their bodies rest there to this day in grave sites that never have been found. No monument stands to their memory.

---

[1] Henry Whittemore, *The Heroes of the American Revolution and their Descendants*, The Heroes of the Revolution Publishing Co., 1897, pp. 72-74.
[2] Capt. Francisco Luengo to Gov. Don Jose Masot, May 14, 1818, American State Papers, Military Affairs, Volume 1, p. 711.
[3] Dr. J.B. Rodgers, Personal Account of Jackson's Campaign, quoted by James Parton, *Life of Andrew Jackson*, Volume 2, p. 455.
[4] *Ibid.*
[5] *Ibid.*
[6] *Ibid.*, p. 456.
[7] *Ibid.*
[8] *Ibid.*, pp. 456-457.
[9] Maj. Robert Butler, Adjutant General, to Brig. Gen. Daniel Parker, Adjutant and Inspector General, May 3, 1818, *American State Papers*, Military Affairs, Volume 1, p. 703.
[10] *Ibid.*
[11] Capt. Francisco Luengo to Gov. Don Jose Masot, May 14, 1818.

---

[12] Dr. J.B. Rodgers, Personal Account of Jackson's Campaign, quoted by James Parton, *Life of Andrew Jackson*, Volume 2, p. 457.

[13] *Ibid.*, pp. 457-458.

[14] *Ibid.*, p. 480.

[15] John Henry Eaton and John Reid, *The Life of Major General Jackson*, p. 290.

Chapter Ten

The Death of Robert Ambrister

THE TERROR AND SADNESS MILLY FRANCIS MUST HAVE FELT as she watched the hanging of her father by American troops is impossible to conceive. She had risked the displeasure of her friends and relatives by pleading for the life of a captive soldier, but now her act of kindness had been repaid with one of harshness and cruelty. Her father had received no trial, but had been executed by a general who chose not to watch as his orders were carried out. As Milly knew, the Prophet Francis had been executed in a manner that to the Creeks and Seminoles was cruel and brutal, designed to take away his courage and dignity as a warrior. Americans often wrote of the cruelties inflicted upon their dead by American Indian warriors, but seldom realized that their own actions were viewed as equally cruel by their enemies.

From the time she was 10 years old, Milly had known little more than war, suffering and death. Her father – the writings of sensationalist 19th century chroniclers aside – had never desired the outcome that grew from his movement. Like the Shawnee Prophet that he emulated, Josiah Francis had wanted peace and prosperity for his people through a return to traditional ways. He believed that if the Creeks gave up the ways of the whites, they could create a paradise for themselves. He remains one of the most misunderstood major figures in American history.

Milly knew the truth about her father and had witnessed his moments of both success and disaster. She knew the disappointment he had felt when his movement collapsed on itself and she saw him return from England burdened with discouragement because the British who had promised so much had failed to keep their promises. The war that cost him his life had not been his idea and, in fact, he had counseled against it. He wanted only to live in peace with his family on the banks of the Wakulla River, but never had the chance.

Horrified by the executions, Milly and her sister went home to their town as the American army marched away on the morning of April 8, 1818. Soldiers were left to hold the fort, where elderly Alexander Arbuthnot was now imprisoned, but the inhabitants of the Prophet's town probably breathed a sad sigh of relief when the main army headed out without destroying their homes.

Jackson pushed east for Boleck's town at present-day Old Town on the Suwannee River. Along the way his troops stumbled into Peter McQueen's force near the Natural Bridge of the Econfina River. The Creek auxiliaries under Brigadier General William McIntosh launched the attack and, supported by additional soldiers from Tennessee, forced McQueen to retreat. The battle was severe and the bodies of 36 Red Sticks were found dead on the ground. Elizabeth Stewart, the only female survivor of the Scott Massacre of 1817, was rescued during the fighting.[1]

Among the children in McQueen's group that day was a young boy about 14-years-old then known as Billy Powell. He later became the "Black Drink Crier" or Asi Yahola of the Alachua Seminoles, a title that has been Anglicized to the better known Osceola. Since even children took up arms to fight the American army, the Battle of Econfina Natural Bridge may well have been Osceola's first battle in defense of his adopted land of Florida.[2]

Milly Francis and Billy Powell (or Osceola) were of about the same age and the bands of their fathers had been closely allied, so they were at least passing acquaintances. Since Peter McQueen, Osceola's maternal uncle, was a friend of the Prophet Josiah Francis, it is logical that the two young people knew each other in Alabama long before their flight to Florida. Along with Tecumseh, William Weatherford, Andrew Jackson and her own father, the future Seminole leader Osceola was among the individuals of note who passed, at least briefly, through the life of Milly Francis.

From the Battle of Econfina, Jackson continued east and attacked Boleck's town on April 16, 1818. As Kenhajo had done at Miccosukee, Boleck fought a brief delaying action while the women and children escaped across the Suwannee River. Casualties were light and the main body of the Seminoles melted away into the wilderness. A large colony of Africans, later to be called "Black Seminoles", was associated with Boleck's town. They fought desperately against Jackson's oncoming troops before falling back across the river with Boleck's Seminoles.

Raiding parties once again went out to capture lingering warriors, confiscate supplies and destroy outlying settlements. One of these pushed down the river and managed to capture not only Alexander Arbuthnot's schooner, the *Chance*, but the former British lieutenant Robert C. Ambrister. He was taken prisoner and sent back to Fort St. Marks, to which Jackson and part of the army returned after completely destroying the Seminole and African settlements along the Suwannee. The Georgia troops, including Duncan McCrimmon, marched overland from Boleck's town back to the settled areas of Georgia, their involvement in the First Seminole War now over.[3]

Upon his return to Fort St. Marks, General Jackson ordered that Arbuthnot and Ambrister be tried for what he viewed as their crimes against the United States. The former was charged with exciting the Creek Indians to war against the United States in violation of the neutrality of Great Britain; acting as a spy and aiding, abetting and comforting the enemy, while supplying them with arms and ammunition; encouraging the Indians to murder William Hambly and Edmund Doyle, as well as seizing their property. Ambrister was charged with aiding, abetting and comforting the enemy even though he was a citizen and former officer of Great Britain, a country then at peace with the United States, and leading and commanding American Indian warriors in their war against the United States.[4]

Jackson ordered that the two be tried before a military court:

The following Detail will compose a Special Court, to convene at this Post, at the hour of 12 o'clock, A.M. for the purpose of investigating the charges exhibited against A. Arbuthnot, Robert Christy Ambrister, and such others who are similarly situated, as may be brought before it. The Court will record all the Documents and Testimony in the several Cases, and their opinion as to the guilt or innocence of the Prisoner, and what punishment (if any) should be inflected.[5]

Named to the court were Major General Edmund P, Gaines, President, and Colonel King, Lieutenant Colonel Gibson, Major Montgomery, Colonel Dyer, Lieutenant Colonel Elliot, Major Minton, Colonel Williamson, Major Muhlenburg, Major Fanning, Captain Crittenden and Lieutenant J.M. Glassell, Recorder.[6]

Both men were tried and both were found guilty of the charges made against them. Neither was afforded a lawyer, as would be normal procedure today, and their trials took place on the soil of a foreign nation, Spain. The court initially sentenced both to death, but upon reconsideration, changed its mind and recommended that they be subjected to lesser punishments. General Jackson, however, disagreed and ordered that both be executed.

He later explained his reasons in a Memorial to Congress, pointing out that Ambrister had "appeared before St. Marks with 4 or 500 under his command" to demand that the Spanish turn the fort over to him. They had refused and he had not forced the issue, but Jackson used the incident as grounds for ordering the executions of both men:

Acting as Chiefs of the Negroes and Indians, Arbuthnot and Ambrister, by numerous acts of atrocity, had become identified with those monsters; - associates in the War. They were the principal authors of the hostilities of the ferocious Savages, who observed none of the rules of civilized warfare; who never gave quarter, and only took prisoners for the purpose of torturing![7]

In his defense of his actions, Jackson did not mention that Milly Francis, a member of the tribe of "ferocious Savages" against whom he had battled, had saved the life of an American soldier. Her demonstration of mercy to Duncan McCrimmon and the decision of his captors to spare his life stood in stark contrast to the acts carried out by other Red Sticks at the Scott Massacre, to which the general made reference in his Memorial.

Jackson also justified to Congress the executions of Josiah Francis and Homathlemico:

...One of the former was a prophet, who had employed his superstitious influence, and the promises of his transatlantic friends, to stimulate his deluded brethren to deeds of rapine and massacre. The other commanded in person the party who perpetrated the cold blooded butchery of Lieutenant Scott, and his unfortunate companions. Both had been engaged in most of the robberies and

murders committed, and were active instigators of the savage War which raged on our defenceless Frontier.[8]

Jackson's assessment of the role of the Prophet Francis in the instigation of the First Seminole War differed significantly from reality, but reflected the general views of whites about what had happened and who was responsible. Although by 1817 he had become an advocate for peace, Francis became a victim of his own reputation from the days of the Creek War of 1813-1814. The mere mention of his name brought back memories of Fort Mims and the horrible battles of that conflict and Jackson judged him based more on the total body of his life than on his true actions in 1817-1818.

The general also defended his decision to overrule his court's reduction of Ambrister's sentence of death:

...In the second Sentence pronounced by the Special Court upon Ambrister, there was a departure from the Rules of Law, upon which alone it was believed jurisdiction was had of the offence. Nor was it less a violation of the Rules and Articles of War; for those rules had denounced corporal punishment. The Sentence, therefore, was void, because known to no Law. Your Respondent, therefore, conceived himself authorized to carry into execution the first Sentence; because it awarded the only punishment that was legal to be inflicted; and because his lawless, guilty, conduct entitled him to die.[9]

Arbuthnot was hanged from the yardarm of his own schooner. Ambrister, in military style, was executed by firing squad.

Dr. J.B. Rodgers, as has been noted, became somewhat familiar with Robert Ambrister at Fort St. Marks. Rodgers had been assigned to care for the sick and wounded American soldiers at the post hospital and during breaks from his duties talked with Ambrister and learned the story of his friendship with Milly Francis. The doctor was among those present to witness the Englishman's death:

"...[H]e straightened himself to his full height, both hands behind him, holding his hat, and being evidently able to see his executioners from under the bandage on his eyes. The signal was immediately given. The platoon fired, some shots taking effect in the head and others about the region of the heart. Ambrister fell forward and died without a struggle.[10]

Rodgers was not the only witness to the shooting of Robert Cristy Ambrister. Drawn to the fort by curiosity, Milly Francis had just arrived when she saw the detail march Ambrister to the place selected for his death:

Among the spectators of the executions was a girl of seventeen who seemed to be in deep distress, and to have no one to comfort her. It was no other than Milly, the daughter of the prophet Francis, who had been so summarily hanged twenty days before. There was white blood in the veins of this beautiful maiden, as there was in those of her father. She was a brunette, with long flowing hair, keen black eyes, and finely-formed person. She was dressed in the manner of white women.[11]

Milly and several others had just reached the bridge of the fort when they saw the soldiers coming, Ambrister among them:

As she was about to cross the bridge over the ditch surrounding the fort, she with the others met the platoon in charge of Ambrister, and not being able to divine the cause of the cortege, stood and witnessed the execution of Ambrister. At this, it was said, she was much distressed, possibly more than at that of her father. It was said by the commandant's family, that Malee went to their house, and there gave full vent to her feelings.[12]

For the second time in as many months, Milly Francis watched in shock as white soldiers executed someone close to her. She had been present when her father died at the end of a rope and now was on hand to see her friend and companion die in a hail of bullets from an American firing squad. It must have seemed to her that she lived a life marked by tragedy. According to Dr. Rodgers, she spoke to none of the Americans and would not answer the inquiries of William Hambly, going instead to the home of the Spanish commandant to seek consolation from his daughters.

---

[1] Dale Cox, *The Scott Massacre of 1817*, pp. 107-114.
[2] *Ibid.*
[3] *Ibid.*, pp. 129-131.
[4] *Ibid.*
[5] Maj. Gen. Andrew Jackson, General Orders of April 26, 1818, issued by Robert Butler, Adjutant General, *British and Foreign State Papers*, Volumes 6-7, p. 792.
[6] *Ibid.*

[7] Andrew Jackson, "The Memorial of Andrew Jackson, Major General in the Army of The United States, and Commander of the Southern Division," March 6, 1820, *British and Foreign State Papers*, Volumes 6-7, pp. 758-777.

[8] *Ibid.*

[9] *Ibid.*

[10] Dr. J.B. Rodgers, Eyewitness Account of Jackson's 1818 Campaign, quoted by James Parton, *Life of Andrew Jackson*, Volume 2, pp. 477-478.

[11] *Ibid.*, p. 480.

[12] *Ibid.*, pp. 482-483.

Photographs

Milly Francis marker at Fort Gadsden Historic Site

Marker at Fort Gadsden Historic Site

105

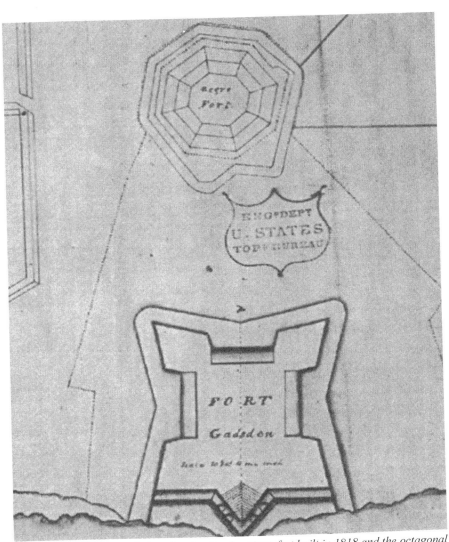

Ground Plan of Fort Gadsden, showing the American fort built in 1818 and the octagonal citadel and magazine of the "Negro Fort."

19th Century sketch of Milly Francis pleading for the life of Duncan McCrimmon

Approximate site of the rescue of McCrimmon by Milly Francis

British flag flying over San Marcos de Apalache, similar to one used to decoy the Prophet

View looking south to site where McKeever decoyed the chiefs aboard his ship

Photographs

Hunting shirt of the Prophet Francis, now at the British Museum
©Trustees of the British Museum

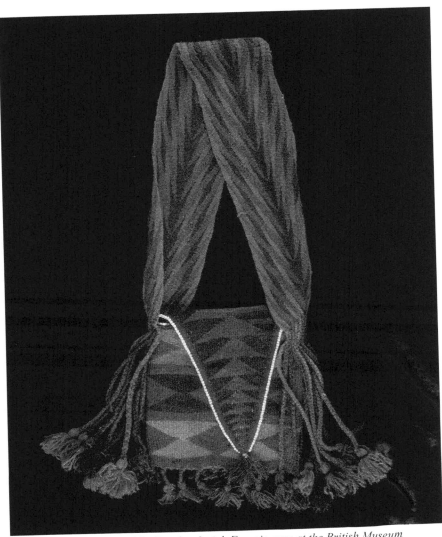

Beaded Pouch of the Prophet Josiah Francis, now at the British Museum
©Trustees of the British Museum.

19th century sketch of the Prophet Francis being brought ashore

General area where the executions of the Prophet Francis and Homathlemico took place.

Milly Francis Monument at San Marcos de Apalache Historic State Park.

Death mask and facial reconstruction of Osceola, on display at Paynes Prairie Preserve.

Lake Miccosukee, women and children waded across to escape Jackson's troops.

Suwannee River, near site of Ambrister's capture.

19th Century sketch of the Trial of Robert Ambrister at San Marcos de Apalache.

Ruins of San Marcos de Apalache, where Ambrister was held prisoner.

Chapter Eleven

The Proposal of Duncan McCrimmon

MOST MEMBERS OF THE "FIVE CIVILIZED TRIBES" BEGAN THEIR JOURNEYS on the Trail of Tears in 1836. For Milly Francis, however, her tragic journey started much earlier. Forced from her home at Holy Ground in 1813, she lived the life of a refugee for much of the rest of her life. As Jackson claimed victory in the First Seminole War, Milly and her family were ordered to leave their home on the Wakulla and move back to the Creek Nation in Alabama.

Although the United States had no legal authority over the inhabitants of Spanish Florida, General Jackson issued orders that the surrendering Red Sticks should be sent back to the Nation. Milly surrendered at Fort St. Marks along with 100 other residents of her father's town. Major A.C.W. Fanning, the commanding officer there, ordered them to Fort Gadsden where they would be supplied with provisions for their long walk back to Alabama:

Within a few days one hundred and eighty eight of the hostile Indians from near Soowaney surrendered themselves at this post. Those with others who have surrendered of late in all about three hundred, I have ordered into the nation, and to report to you. They are in a most wretched condition, and will be at Fort Gaines about the sixteenth of next month. I shall make provision for them until the 1st October, or until I hear from you, or some arrangements is made for them, provided that may be soon.[1]

Once again, Milly's family and friends were reduced to abject poverty. All of their possessions other than those they could carry on their own backs were lost when they began their walk to Fort Gadsden. Food was in short supply and hunger stalked them as they made their way west to the Apalachicola River:

...[T]he hostile Indians are in a state of starvation; the warriors are raising the corn which was buried in the ground, and which of course was not destroyed by our troops, and seem determined to recommence the war in the fall. The wife and family of the prophet Francis are among the prisoners: two of his daughters are very interesting young ladies, and speak very good English, as in fact the whole family do except the mother. The eldest, when her father went on board the Thomas Shields, shortly afterwards followed, supposing her to be a British vessel. Before she got along side, however, she discovered the deception, pushed off and effected her escape.[2]

Milly, by the time she arrived at Fort Gadsden in late July 1818, had become something of a celebrity to the American military officers. It was from a letter dated at the fort on August 31, 1818, that the legend of the Creek Pocahontas began to grow:

...The youngest and most beautiful is caressed by all the officers for having saved the life of a Georgia militia man, whom her countrymen had taken prisoner and were about to put to death, when this modern Pocahontas, finding entreaties vain, declared her determination to save his life or perish with him: she was successful, and the man was preserved.[3]

In Milledgeville and elsewhere in Georgia, citizens donated money for the benefit of Milly and her family. Media pressure grew on Duncan McCrimmon to relieve her sufferings:

As long as he remained a prisoner, M'Krimmon's benefactress continued to show him acts of kindness. Now the fortune of war has placed her in the power of the white people, she arrived at Fort Gadsden not long since, with a number of others that had surrendered, in a starving condition. We are gratified to learn, that a proper respect for her virtues induced the commanding officer, Col. Arbuckle, to relieve her immediate wants. M'Krimmon appears to have a due sense of the obligation he owes the woman who saved his life at the hazard of her own – he left town last week to seek her, and as far as may be in his power to alleviate her misfortunes. It is also his firm determination, we understand, if she will consent, to make her his wife, and reside, provided he can prevail upon her to do so, within the settled parts of Georgia.[4]

Newspaper readers across the nation read the story of McCrimmon's planned proposal to Milly Francis and visions of a romance between the two blossomed in the American mind. Few seemed to consider the possibility that Milly might not want to marry a man who had marched in the army that had killed her father and friend and that even now was forcing her from her home on the long trail back to the Creek Nation.

The spread of her story, however, forced white readers and editors to reconsider their long held prejudices against American Indians. Like General Jackson himself, most Americans of that day considered their Indian neighbors to be ruthless savages, who delighted in nothing more than the shedding of blood. Through her act of mercy, Milly Francis challenged such beliefs and although the writings of editors of the time ring as unquestionably racist today, they indicate that the young Creek woman had caused a ripple in the conscience of a nation. The words of a Milledgeville editor provide a good example:

It thus appears, that rude and uncultivated minds are capable of the finest susceptibility, of the warmest attachments, of the most inviolable friendships – and that they sometimes display virtues, which would do credit in a people the most refined and enlightened.[5]

In New Jersey, the editor of the *Trenton Federalist* analyzed his own thoughts about Milly's actions in saving Duncan McCrimmon. He was troubled by the mercy she showed to McCrimmon as opposed to the harsh sentence imposed on her father by General Jackson:

Milly Francis – The distinguished act of humanity which has bro't this young indian woman into public notice, in saving the life of a Georgia militia man, taken prisoner by the Indians, an account of which was published in our paper last week, may be compared with that of General Jackson, but with little credit to the humanizing influence of civilization. Her father, after yielding to her solicitations and sparing the life of his prisoner, contrary o Indian custom, was himself made prisoner by the Americans – and was put to death by order of General Jackson. Francis was decoyed on board one of our vessels by hoisting a British flag instead of that of the United States, and thus was made prisoner – and thus put to death.[6]

As editors of newspapers reconsidered their feelings about American Indians, Duncan McCrimmon made his way back down the Apalachicola River to Fort Gadsden. Because of the regard for which they held Milly, Lieutenant Colonel Matthew Arbuckle and the other officers of the fort allowed her family to remain there where they could be provided with food and other necessities.

McCrimmon reached Fort Gadsden at the end of November of 1818 and his long-anticipated meeting with Milly Francis took place a short time later. Colonel Arbuckle, who was present, described Milly's reaction to the Georgia man's offer of marriage:

Duncan M'Rimmon is here – Milly, the Prophet Francis's daughter, says she saved his life, or used such influence as she possessed to that effect, from feelings of humanity alone, and that she would have rendered the same service to any other white man similarly circumstanced – she is therefore not disposed to accept his offer of matrimony, which has been made as an acknowledgement of gratitude. The donation presented through me (by the citizens of Milledgeville) to Milly, has been delivered, and she manifested a considerable degree of thankfulness for their kindness.[7]

Nearly 25 years later, Milly recalled the day that McCrimmon came to propose marriage to her. Speaking with Colonel Ethan Allen Hitchcock in January 1842, she remembered that, "she refused him, saying, she did not save his life to marry him."[8]

News of Milly's refusal of McCrimmon's proposal was published by newspapers throughout the nation. Instead of the romantic end they expected to report of the story, they now detailed her refusal of his offer in terms that expanded her growing legend. The *Camden Gazette*, for example, described her as a woman "who so generously saved a Georgia militia-man" and reported that she had received, "with much gratitude, a sum of money presented to her by the citizens of Milledgeville." The writer went on to remind readers that "her father was decoyed on board one of our vessels and hung!"[9]

Across the United States, white mothers and fathers named their young daughters "Milly Francis" in recognition of qualities shown by the real Creek Pocahontas. U.S. Census records for the 1800s show that hundreds of little girls were named in Milly's honor. Her name lives on in the family trees of thousands of American citizens who have no connection to her other than a long ago tribute paid by fathers and mothers who were impressed by her act of kindness.

The survivors of the Prophet's family, Milly among them, made their way back up the river to the Creek Nation. They passed through Fort Gaines in Georgia and Fort Mitchell in Alabama as they went, receiving basic supplies from the U.S. Army. By 1819 they were once again in the Creek Nation where they settled near Tuckabatchee and tried to rebuild their home and lives.

---

[1] Lt. Col. Matthew Arbuckle to David B. Mitchell, Agent of the Creek Nation, August 31, 1818, Office of the Adjutant General, Letters Received, 1805-1821, National Archives.
[2] Letter from Fort Gadsden (probably written by Lt. Col. Matthew Arbuckle), August 31, 1818, published in the *Milledgeville Reflector*, October 13, 1818, p. 3.
[3] *Ibid.*
[4] *Milledgeville Reflector*, November 2, 1818.
[5] *Ibid.*
[6] *Trenton Federalist*, Volume XVII, Issue 1034, December 21, 1818, p. 3.
[7] Lt. Col. Matthew Arbuckle to the Editor, December 1, 1818, published in the *Georgia Journal*, December 22, 1818, p. 3.
[8] Ethan Allen Hitchcock, Diary Entry of January 27, 1842, in Grant Foreman, *A Traveler in Indian Country, The Journal of Ethan Allen Hitchcock*, pp. 102-104.
[9] *Camden Gazette*, Volume III, Issue 143, January 7, 1819, p. 3.

Chapter Twelve

The Trail of Tears

THE SEVENTEEN YEARS THAT FOLLOWED THE RETURN OF MILLY FRANCIS to the Creek Nation were the most peaceful of her life. The horrors of war slowly became a distant memory as she made a life for herself among her people. Not long after her return to Alabama she married a Creek warrior named Cochar Hoboithley and the young couple settled in a small cabin at the Hickory Ground, a large and old Creek town in the heart of the surviving portion of the Nation. They began a family and over the next 17 years had eight children.[1]

Little is known of her life during the time of her residence back in the Nation. The 1832 Creek Census shows that she and her husband were living at Hickory Ground with three of their children. Things by then were not going well for the Creeks. Their lands were surrounded by white settlements, farms, towns and cities. Pressure on them to relocate to new lands west of the Mississippi had become intense and frauds and other crimes were being perpetrated against them with alarming frequency.[2]

On January 7, 1832, the principal chiefs of the nation appointed Tuckabatchee Hadjo and Octiarche Emathla to go to Washington, D.C., on their behalf to protest against white intrusions on Creek sovereignty and lands. Paddy and Thomas Carr were appointed as interpreters and Major John H. Broadax was named special agent for the emissaries. Their complaints were numerous and serious:

> ...*Murders have already taken place, both by the reds and whites. We have caused the red men to be brought to justice, the whites go unpunished. We are weak and our words and oaths go for naught; justice we don't expect, nor can we get. We may expect murders to be more frequent.*[3]

In addition the chiefs complained that liquor was being brought into the Nation by whites to allow them to commit frauds and steal land. They were being illegally held subject to state laws that they could not comprehend and never knew when they would be punished under a law they did not understand.[4]

The response of the Secretary of War was that the President was powerless to help them and that they should move to the West for their own safety. Additional chiefs were sent to Washington to try to help with the negotiations, even as additional white settlers poured into the Nation, claiming lands that for the most part had been taken from Creek owners by fraud:

> ...*We have made many treaties with the United States, at all times with a belief that the one making to be the last; but from the great assurance given us for protection, and the frequent solicitations of our great father, we have frequently given up large tracts of our country for a mere song; and we are now called on for the remnant of our land, and for us to remove beyond the Mississippi.*[5]

The Jackson Administration (Andrew Jackson was now the President of the United States) remained adamant that there was little it could do to help the Creeks and that it was in their best interest to relocate to new homes west of the Mississippi. There they would be far away from the white settlers and outlaws causing them so much trouble, would have all the land they needed and would be free to live their lives as they saw fit, or at least so said the U.S. Government.

The Creek delegates must have reflected on the Creek War of 1813-1814 and the destruction it had brought upon their nation. Some of them, however, undoubtedly remembered the teachings of the Prophet Francis and his declarations that if they united, they would be able to repel American intrusions on their lands. They had not united, of course, but had instead fought against each other and now their lands were disappearing from beneath their feet.

Left with little choice, the delegates signed a new treaty with the United States on March 24, 1832. Remembered today as the Treaty of 1832, it ceded away all Creek lands east of the Mississippi River with the proviso that each member of the Nation be given an individual parcel of land that they could occupy for five years unless they decided to sell sooner. This would give them places to live and grow crops until they were ready to make the long journey west to what is now Oklahoma. In return, the United States agreed to remove all intruders from these lands for five years. The U.S. would pay the cost of the trip to the west and provide food for the Creeks for one year after their arrival there until they were able to produce crops of their own. Each warrior would be given a rifle and ammunition and each family a blanket. The treaty stipulated that the new lands west of the Mississippi would be guaranteed to them and that no state or territory of the United States would ever be allowed to exercise control over them.[6]

With the signing of a document, the United States and a small group of Creek leaders condemned 23,596 men, women and children to the horror remembered today as the Trail of Tears. The chiefs, at least, did not realize what they were doing to their people by placing their marks on the treaty, but they soon learned.

The Treaty of 1832 allocated $100,000 to pay any outstanding debts of the Creeks. This provision caused immediate and unsettling trouble. White speculators flooded into the nation to sell merchandise and liquor on credit at exorbitant prices. The Secretary of War ordered them removed, but with as much regard to their feelings as possible. It was a toothless directive and in September 1832 the Creek leaders once again complained to Washington. "Instead of our situation being relieved as was anticipated," they wrote, "we are distressed in a ten fold manner – we are surrounded by the whites with their fields and fences, our lives are in jeopardy, we are daily threatened."[7]

The situation in the Creek Nation was deteriorating and continued to deteriorate over the next four years. Investigations were conducted by the U.S. government – one even headed by Francis McHenry, author of "The Star-Spangled Banner" – but no good came of them.

Resistance grew in a large faction of the Creeks, particularly the Yuchi and Hitchiti who lived in the lower towns. They were upset over the signing away of their lands by the chiefs who had gone to Washington in 1832. As time passed and the frauds and crimes committed against them grew in severity, they decided that they would not leave without a fight. Among their leaders was Neamathla (Eneah Emathla), the same old chief – now in his 80s – who had taken part in the first battle of the Seminole Wars when he resisted a U.S. Army attempt to surround Fowltown in Southwest Georgia. He later was forced again to give up his home at present-day Tallahassee so that a capital city for the new Territory of Florida could be built there. Disgusted, Neamathla took his people and moved up to the Creek Nation where by the 1830s he was the principal chief of Hitchiti.

Milly Francis likely viewed these events with growing alarm and trepidation. Conflict and crime were rampant. White speculators and conmen had flooded into her Nation and it appeared that she and her family soon would be forced to move far away to a place they had never seen. Then, in the spring of 1836, war erupted in the Creek Nation.

Led by Neamathla, Neah Micco, Jim Henry (later James McHenry) and others, the Hitchiti and Yuchi – joined by some Muskogees – rose up against the whites. The Georgia town of Roanoke, built on lands taken from the Creeks, was burned to the ground and a number of its defenders killed. Travelers and settlers in the Nation were attacked, their scalped bodies left to litter the roads and pathways that led from Georgia into Creek country. The conflict is known today as the Creek War of 1836 and like the earlier war waged by Josiah Francis and the Red Sticks, it created near panic in the white settlements bordering the nation. Residents fled their homes and communities to points of safety. Even the growing city of Columbus feared attack at any minute and the local militia was called out.

Employing the same strategy used in 1813-1814, white armies marched on the Creeks from different directions. The Georgia army, led by Major General Winfield T. Scott, slowly assembled at Columbus and then marched down the east side of the Chattahoochee River to Roanoke. The Alabama army, led by Brigadier General Thomas S. Jessup, did the lion's share of putting down the uprising by marching directly on the Hitchiti and Yuchi, capturing Neamathla and other leaders and forcing the surrender of their followers. Fort Mitchell, on the Alabama side of the Chattahoochee River just below Columbus, became a holding pen into which the surrendered Creeks were herded.

The uprising was a desperate last stand by a portion of the Creeks to defend their remaining lands. The United States used it, however, as a pretense to begin what some have called the "American Holocaust." The Creeks across the Nation were ordered to assemble at emigration (i.e. concentration) camps to prepare to begin their journeys west. Protests that one full year still remained of the five years promised to them by the Treaty of 1832 were to no avail.

Milly Francis and her children were among the 1,984 men, women and children who assembled at Tallassee on the Tallapoosa River for removal on the Trail of Tears. The principal chief of their party was Tuckabatchee Hadjo, who used "every argument against it" to Lieutenant J.T. Sprague of the U.S. Marines.

His people had not had time to sell their cattle or gather their belongings, he explained, but his pleas were of no use. Tuckabatchee Hadjo was compelled to go.[8]

Milly's husband, Cochar Hoboithley, was not with her and the children when they were told to assemble at Tallassee for the journey west. He had enlisted in a regiment of Creek soldiers formed by the United States to assist against the Seminoles in Florida. A private in Company E of the First Battalion, he saw action at the noted Battle of Wahoo Swamp, where Milly's cousin – Major David B. Moniac – was killed. The son of her uncle Samuel Moniac, the major was the first American Indian to graduate from the U.S. Military Academy at West Point.[9]

Lieutenant Sprague served as the commander of the military escort that supervised the move of the party that included Milly and her children. The actual work of supplying the Creeks on the journey was contracted to the Alabama Emigrating Company. Much is known about Milly's route on the Trail of Tears because Lieutenant Sprague kept a detailed journal of the march. Like most whites of his day, he believed that relocating thousands of American Indians from their homes and lands east of the Mississippi was for their own good. "In this state of things, however indignant their feelings, or however great the sacrifice," he wrote, "it was but justice to get them out of the country as soon as possible."[10]

The Trail of Tears for Milly Francis had begun long before, but its final act was initiated on September 5, 1836. Placing the heartbroken men, women and children into the care of Felix G. Gibson and Charles Abercrombie of the Alabama Emigrating Company, Sprague started them on the long march west:

...The train consisted of forty-five waggons of every description, five hundred ponies and two thousand Indians. The moving of so large a body necessarily required some days to effect an arrangement to meet the comfort and convenience of all. The marches for the first four or five days were long and tedious and attended with many embarrassing circumstances. Men, who had ever had claims upon these distressed beings, now preyed upon them without mercy. Fraudulent demands were presented and unless some friend was near, they were robbed of their horses and even clothing.[11]

In some cases Creek warriors had to use violence to protect themselves and the women and children from robbery. Sprague resorted to "forced marches" to get them out of the former Creek Nation as quickly as possible, fearing that unless he did so the outraged warriors would have wreaked "their vengeance upon the innocent as well as the guilty."[12]

As the long march began, Sprague immediately noticed that "from their natural indolence and utter disregard for the future" many of the people under his supervision began to straggle in hopes of being left behind. They were willing to beg, steal or find what food they could just so they could remain in their own country. It never occurred to the lieutenant that the reason for their straggling was a sincere and deep attachment to a homeland that was being taken from them. He threatened to put them in irons or call in soldiers to compel their movement. Such threats had, he reported, a "salutary effect."[13]

The party reached Town Creek, Alabama, on September 24, 1836, having marched an average of around 12 miles per day for 20 days. They continued on the next morning, beginning a stretch of the journey that was even more harsh and difficult. Like the other members of the party, Milly and the children suffered from lack of water during long walks that sometimes extended as far as 20 miles in a single day. Food was in short supply:

...Great inconvenience was experienced upon this entire route for the want of Depots of provisions. There was no time when the proper rations were not issued, but from the frequent necessity of gathering and hauling corn, the Indians were often obliged to take their rations after dark. This caused great confusion and many were deprived of their just share.[14]

The party reached Memphis on October 7, 1836. The steamboats they expected to carry them on the rest of their journey were nowhere to be seen. After giving them one day to rest, Sprauge moved the Creeks across the Mississippi River to West Memphis where they camped in the mud along the riverbanks. Other "emigrating" parties had arrived at Memphis as well and Sprague reported that 13,000 American Indians were camped there, exposed to the elements and to great misery. Fortunately for Milly and the children, the long-awaited steamboats finally arrived on October 11th:

The Mississippi Swamp at this season was impassable for waggons and it was agreed that the horses should go through while the women and children with their baggage took steamboats to Rock Roe. This place was attained by descending the Mississippi, about one hundred miles to the mouth of White River, and ascending this river about seventy miles, thereby avoiding a swamp about fifty miles in breadth.[15]

The Spanish conquistador Hernando de Soto had died of fever in the swamps of the Arkansas Delta and many members of Tuckabatchee Hadjo's party of Creeks did as well. Death and misery had become a daily scene along the Trail of Tears.

The plan to carry the women and children up the White River quickly fell apart due to delays in the embarkation of the parties in line ahead of Sprague's. He met with the chiefs and contractors and agreement was reached to carry them instead up the Arkansas River to Little Rock:

> ...The advantages to be gained by this were evident; it put us ahead of all the other parties, secured us an abundant supply of provisions, and avoided a tedious journey of one hundred and fifty miles on foot. A commodious steam boat was procured and upon this and two flat boats I put as near as could be estimated fifteen hundred women and children and some men, with their baggage. The men amounting to some six or seven hundred passed through the swamp with their horses, in charge of my Assistant Agent Mr. Freeman.[16]

Milly and her children, with the other women and children, traveled to Little Rock aboard the steamboat *John Nelson* or one of the barges it towed. The Arkansas River was running high and the journey was slow and perilous, but they were at least provided with bacon and corn and the boat stopped each night to allow them time to cook. Along the way they passed Arkansas Post, where the last battle of the American Revolution had been fought on April 17, 1783. The site is now a national memorial.

The boats reached Little Rock on October 3, 1836, and the men who trudged through the mud of the swamp arrived the next day:

> ...Many remained behind and sent word, that "when they had got bear skins enough to cover them they would come on." Here, they felt independent, game was abundant, and they were almost out of the reach of the white-men. At first, it was my determination to remain at Little Rock until the whole party should assemble. But from the scarcity of provisions and the sale of liquor, I determined to proceed up the country about fifty miles and there await the arrival of all the Indians. Tuck-e-batch-e-hadjo refused to go. "He wanted nothing from the white-men and should rest."[17]

Sprague accused the chief of being drunk and after a brief halt at Little Rock, moved the party out to continue its journey up the Arkansas River. The camp there was at what is now North Little Rock, along the banks of the river and within sight of the old Arkansas State House which still stands today. The men women and children – Milly among them – once again boarded the steamboat to continue their journey up the Arkansas. They reached Potts Inn near Lewisburg, Arkansas, on October 10, 1836. It was there that Lieutenant Sprague learned that some of the men from the overland party were refusing to leave the vast swamps between the Mississippi and White Rivers:

...A body of Indians under a secondary Chief, Narticher-tus-ten-nugge expressed their determination to remain in the swamp in spite of every remonstrance. They evinced the most hostile feelings and cautioned the white-men to keep away from them.[18]

Straggling was increasing, as was sickness, death and misery. The size of the party diminished as those unable to keep up were simply left behind to find their way. Members of Tuckabatchee Hadjo's party were freezing in bitter cold at Potts Inn as late as December of that year. To assist them on their way, the Governor of Arkansas sent militia troops to drive them out.

To try to save at least some of the elderly and sick, Sprague placed them aboard a chartered steamboat and ordered it up to Fort Gibson, which stood in present-day Oklahoma near the line of the new territory assigned to the Creeks. The boat arrived there on October 22, 1836.

The others, including Milly and the children, suffered through winter's first blast as they began their journey by foot up the road along the side of the Arkansas River:

The sufferings of the Indians at this period were intense. With nothing more than a cotton garment thrown over them, their feet bare, they were compelled to encounter cold, sleeting storms and to travel over hard frozen ground. Frequent appeals were made to me to clothe their nakedness and protect their lacerated feet.[19]

Sprague had neither clothing nor shoes to give them and could do little more than point to the provisions of the contract which included no commitment to supply them with such. He halted the march on October 22, 1836, to give the people time to rest and warm themselves, but the halt only increased their suffering. They moved out again on the 23rd, the weather still severe.

They camped near Spadra the next day and were preparing for another day of misery on the road when the steamboat was seen coming down the river on its return from Fort Gibson. The party now amounted to around 1,600 people and Sprague crammed all but a few of them onto the boat and started it for Fort Gibson the next morning. Milly and the children were likely aboard the steamer. Sprague accompanied the land party, all of whom were now mounted or in wagons and moving forward as fast as humanly possible:

...On the 30th we learned that owing to the rapid fall of the Arkansas the boat had grounded. We soon came in the vicinity of her; wagons were procured and this body from the boat soon joined those on shore. The Indians here were frequently intoxicated. They procured liquor from other Indians residents of the country, and the artifices of both combined no man could detect.[20]

The grounding of the boat probably took place somewhere near Fort Smith and Milly Francis likely gained her first sight of the land reserved for the "Five Civilized Tribes" as she either walked or rode in a wagon in that vicinity. The country of the Cherokee Nation, which they were obliged to cross to reach Fort Gibson, is quite beautiful and defies the stereotypical expectation of Oklahoma's terrain. The Boston Mountains, part of the magnificent Ozark chain, stretch across the Arkansas line on the north side of the river, while to the south the high ridges of the Ouachitas can be seen. Prairies and forests then covered the landscape. In appearance, it was not far removed from the Talladega Mountains of the old Creek Nation in Alabama.

The terrain gradually changed, becoming more open and level and the party arrived within 17 miles of Fort Gibson on December 7, 1836. Milly and the others reached the fort the next day and were ordered by Brigadier General Matthew Arbuckle to establish a camp near the stockade. Arbuckle was the same officer who had battled Neamathla back in 1817 and was part of Jackson's army when Milly's father was hanged at St. Marks in 1818. He also had shown mercy to Milly and her family at Fort Gadsden and was present when she declined Duncan McCrimmon's marriage proposal. It is not known if he was aware of her presence at his post in 1836.[21]

Milly Francis received the one blanket promised for her entire family on December 20, 1836, and then joined the others on a final two-day march into the territory reserved for them by the government in Washington, D.C. Thirty-five miles from Fort Gibson, Lieutenant Sprague halted them on a prairie. Their long journey west was over. "They soon scattered in every direction," he reported, "seeking a desirable location for their new homes."[22]

Twenty-nine members of Sprague's party, most of them children, died on the Trail of Tears. Others were so sick and enfeebled by the journey that they did not long survive their arrival in the new Creek Nation:

...To say they were not in a distressed and wretched condition, would be in contradiction to the well known history of the Creeks for the last two years. They were poor, wretchedly, and depravedly poor, many of them without a garment to cover their nakedness...They left their country, at a warm season of the year, thinly clad, and characteristically indifferent to their rapid approach to regions of a climate to which they were unaccustomed, they expended what little they had for intoxicating drinks or for some gaudy article of jewelry.[23]

While Sprague's comments reflect some of the biases of his day, they do accurately describe the condition of the people in Tuckabatchee Hadjo's party when they reached their new country during the winter of 1836-1837. No homes awaited them. They had no fresh supplies of clothing or shoes. Provisions were issued to them, but often were delayed or did not come at all. The suffering of that first winter in present-day Oklahoma is immense.

Some of the chiefs and leading men of Cusseta, who were part of Sprague's party, delivered a bitter letter to the lieutenant on December 21, 1836. They reminded him that he had "heard the cries of our women and children" and watched in person as they "laid the bones of our men, women and children" in graves along the way. The horses they had been promised they could keep were gone. "We wanted to gather our crops, and we wanted to go in peace and friendship," they wrote. "Did we?" the letter continued, "No! We were drove off like wolves."[24]

Driven into her new country like an animal, Milly Francis took her children and found a plot of land not far across the Grand River from Fort Gibson. There, with help from family and neighbors, she built a small cabin on the site of today's Bacone College to shelter herself and the children for the winter and to await the arrival of her husband from the war against the Seminoles.

[1] Maj. W.G. Freeman, "Muster Roll of deceased officers and soldiers of the Mounted Regiment of Creek Indian Volunteers," September 28, 1837, Senate Executive Document 44, 30th Congress, 1st Session, 1848.

[2] Creek Nation Census of 1832, Certified May 1 and May 13, 1833, Senate Document 512, 23rd Congress, 1st Session.

[3] Eneah Micco and other chiefs to the Secretary of War, April 8, 1831, Office of Indian Affairs, "Creek Emigration," Document II, p. 424.

[4] *Ibid.*

[5] Document III

[6] Treaty of 1832.

[7] Document III, p. 464.

[8] Journal of Lt. J.T. Sprague, included in Sprague to Harris, April 1, 1837, OIA, "Creek Emigration" file.

[9] Maj. W.G. Freeman, "Muster Roll of deceased officers and soldiers of the Mounted Regiment of Creek Indian Volunteers, September 28, 1837, Senate Executive Document 55, 30th Congress, 1st Session, 1848.

[10] Journal of Lt. J.T. Sprague.

[11] *Ibid.*

[12] *Ibid.*

[13] *Ibid.*

[14] *Ibid.*

[15] *Ibid.*

[16] *Ibid.*

[17] *Ibid.*

[18] *Ibid.*

[19] *Ibid.*

[20] *Ibid.*

[21] *Ibid.*

[22] *Ibid.*

[23] *Ibid.*

[24] Kasitah Chiefs to Lt. J.T. Sprague, December 21, 1836, enclosed in Sprague to Harris, April 1, 1837, OIL, "Creek Emigration" file.

Chapter Thirteen

The Medal of Honor

UPON HER ARRIVAL IN THE WEST, Milly must have longed for the help, support and companionship of her husband. He was still far away in Florida, serving the cause of those who had subjected his wife, children, family and friends to such great misery. He had no way of knowing the conditions to which they had been subjected, of course, but there was little he could have done even if he had known.

It is impossible to know how many people from the Creek Nation died during that first brutal year in the West. Milly was fortunate to survive, as was her youngest child – a boy of about seven years of age. She had no money and no means. Her neighbors and extended family helped, but they were in similar circumstances and there was little they could do. The one blanket given to her family by the government did little to stave off the cold of the raw Oklahoma winter and spring. The old chief Neamathla, the same leader who had been attacked by U.S. troops in 1817 sparking the First Seminole War had been marched west on the Trail of Tears following his capture in Alabama. He now protested to the government that it had failed to provide the people with the tools, provisions and in many cases even the blankets they had been promised. His pleas were to no avail.

Things grew even worse as thousands of other Creeks reached the new territory. Conditions were deplorable and sickness prevailed. As those already in the Nation tried to care for the new arrivals, supply lines stretched to the breaking point and broke. Hunger and death stalked the Creeks. Colonel Arbuckle and other officers at Fort Gibson could do little to relieve their suffering. There were too many people for the supplies on hand. Neither could the neighboring Cherokee do much to help. A portion of that nation had migrated west ahead of the Trail of Tears, but now was swamped with the forced emigration inflicted upon their own people.

History records that in 1836-1837, tens of thousands of American Indian men, women and children were driven from their homes and forced west on the Trail of Tears. Thousands died. The human cost of forced removal is impossible to conceive and the total number of deaths will never be known.

Milly Francis waited in vain during the spring and summer of 1837 for the arrival of her husband. Cochar Hoboithley had joined other warriors in forming the Creek Regiment of Mounted Volunteers that served the United States in the Second Seminole War. They had enrolled on September 1, 1836 and been mustered into the U.S. Army on the 18th of that month. Under the command of Milly's cousin Major David Moniac – the first American Indian to graduate from the U.S. Military Academy at West Point – Cochar Hoboithley had fought most notably at the Battle of Wahoo Swamp on November 21, 1836.

The Seminoles there had taken up positions on the west bank of a swampy stream known today as Battle Branch. The U.S. Army approached from the east, but found itself unable to cross the stream because the Seminoles unleashed withering volleys of rifle fire each time the soldiers moved into the open. Uncertainty over the depth of the water kept the troops from attacking the Seminole position en masse. A frustrated Major Moniac decided to break the stalemate and led some of the Creeks forward but he was shot down and killed just as he waded into the stream. Unwilling to sacrifice his men to useless slaughter, General (and Governor) Richard Keith Call ordered them to retreat, leaving the victorious Seminoles in command of the field. The water later was found to be shallow enough to cross.

Cochar Hoboithley survived the fight at Wahoo Swamp, as well as his regiment's other service in Florida. With the other Creek volunteers he boarded ship to begin his own journey west in mid-1837. The warriors went first to Mobile Point and from there on to Pass Christian, Mississippi. By the time the Creeks reached the Pass, they were suffering from a severe outbreak of sickness. Twenty-three men from the regiment died at Pass Christian. Cochar Hoboithley was among them. The husband of Milly Francis died of sickness on July 26, 1837.[1]

How much Milly Francis ever learned of her husband's service and death is not known. She was told of his passing by other members of his regiment as they reached the new Creek Nation during the winter of 1837-1838. Her situation by then had become desperate. Living in a small dirt-floored cabin on a hill overlooking the confluence of the Arkansas, Neosho and Verdigras Rivers, she grew a small garden and did all she could to survive. Her life was difficult and from the time of her arrival in the west until her death ten years later she suffered from hunger, sickness and misery.

Milly's home stood on the campus of today's Bacone College, which was founded in 1880 as the Indian University. In continuous operation since the day of its founding, Bacone is the oldest active institution of higher learning in Oklahoma. A monument to Milly Francis stands on the grounds of the school, which is located atop elevated ground south of the confluence of the Arkansas with the Verdigras and Neosho Rivers. The site is within the sharp bend where the flow of the Arkansas turns from almost due east to almost due south to wrap around today's city of Muskogee. It is only about four miles from Fort Gibson, the military post commanded by Colonel Matthew Arbuckle at the time of Milly's arrival.

When Milly settled here in 1837, she likely did so because the fort was the point from which provisions and other supplies were issued to the Creeks. In addition, the hilltop was adjacent to the broad floodplain of the confluence, which offered rich soil for farming and timber for building and firewood. Hoping to profit from trade with the Creeks as they established themselves in their new lands and slowly grew more prosperous, Seaborn Hill established a store on the same side of the Arkansas River about one-mile from the cabin of Milly Francis. This provided her with another source of supply, although money was in short supply.

In 1841-1842, Lieutenant Colonel Ethan Allen Hitchcock was assigned by the government to investigate reports of frauds committed on the newly emigrants. The evidence was widespread and overwhelming, as was shown by Neamathla's pleading to the colonel:

...Enehenathla, a chief, tells me that towards the close of the year one of the agents came to him and said, "You have now raised corn and have enough to live on: you had better sell your rations claim." There was three months' rations due, he says, and he and his people received $1.50 in money for each claim – only

$1.50 for three months' rations! Account 3 X 30, 90 rations X 12 ½ cents: $11.25. So the contractors put into their own pockets $9.75 for each!!![2]

Neamathla had good reason to complain. Based on Hitchcock's computation, he and his people had received only $1.50 each for rations worth $11.25 each. The agents had stolen more than 90% of the value of the rations from the Creeks.

The old Red Stick was not alone in his complaints. From the time he reached Fort Gibson on January 16, 1842, Colonel Hitchcock heard stories of frauds and illegalities being perpetrated on the Creeks and Cherokees. He found cases of white men who arrived in the Nations broke or as much as $20,000 in debt but who became wealthy through their dealings with the Indians. On January 21st, having been recommended to him, Hitchcock had dinner with Seaborn Hill and his family. He learned that Hill had spoken publicly about frauds being committed on the Creeks by the government contractors. A contractor named Harrison challenged him to a duel with rifles at 40 yards and then Bowie knives at close quarters should they miss or not do fatal injury with the rifles. An army officer intervened and put a stop to the duel before it could take place.[3]

Hitchcock's journal describes horse races at Fort Gibson with bets as high as $500. He also described how quickly liquor was spreading among the depressed emigrants. White traders sold it by the jug to Indian traders who then sold it drop by drop to their own people:

Among other sights today I saw a knot of whiskey sellers – women whiskey sellers. I stumbled upon a knot of people who did not know me and saw a young squaw, not old or ugly either, but rather young and good looking, with her left hand so doubled up as to conceal under a shawl a bottle of whiskey from which she was selling by a small tin cup a gill or two gills at a time – a bit a gill. As she emptied her bottle she would go to a clump of bushes near where an older and uglier squaw merchant had a gallon jug from which the bottle was filled. I saw two or three others selling also. The day was very fine and clear for the season. Truly God sends his sunshine upon the just and unjust, the godly and ungodly.[4]

Hitchcock urged the commander of Fort Gibson to shut down the horse races and gambling at the fort. He had seen wealthy men taking the last dime from destitute Creek and Cherokee Indians. The commandant – Colonel Mason – agreed and posted notice that gambling was prohibited at the post. He also required newly arriving whites to register at the fort and to state their business.

Exasperated at his inability to stop the gambling and drinking around the post, he finally ordered the closure of a tavern that was at the center of the conduct.[5]

The colonel once again crossed over to Seaborn Hill's place on January 27, 1842. There he met with Benjamin Marshall and other Creek leaders who proved to him that rations allocated for the Creek people had been short by 25%. They also reported that $8,000 of their $31,900 annuity for 1837 had never been paid, despite the passage of five years.

These frauds involving rations and the annuity money due to the Creeks had real and dire impacts on families like that of Milly Francis. They arrived in the new territory hungry, cold and all but naked. Then, while they tried to survive until they could grow their crops during the summer of 1837, white speculators and officers had deprived them of desperately needed food and money. It is no wonder that so many Creek men, women and children died during their first year in Oklahoma.

On the afternoon of the 27th, Hitchcock rode with Mr. Hill from his home on the north side of the Arkansas River to his store on the opposite shore. He had heard mention that Milly lived nearby and that she had made a claim for eight slaves then living among the Seminoles. Using her claim as an opportunity to meet her and hear the story of how she had saved Duncan McCrimmon, Colonel Hitchcock sent for her and asked her to visit him at Hill's store. Since her home was only one mile away, it was not long before she arrived:

...Milly is now over 45 & a widow in this country, living a mile from the Hills store on the South side of the Arkansas some 2 or 3 miles from the mouth of the Grand River. She has two sons and a daughter living of eight children, was dressed something like a white woman as I saw her today...She came in with her eldest boy about 14 or 15. She is fairer than Indian women generally as her father was of mixed blood.[6]

Hitchcock wrote in pencil as Milly explained the details of the slave issue to him. Although her account was a little confused due to the passage of time, she told him that when her father left to go to England in 1815, he had divided some of his slaves among his children, giving one woman to Milly. Her sister sent them south deeper into Florida with the Seminoles at about the time of her father's execution. They never were returned.[7]

Not long after she arrived in the new territory, Milly told Hitchcock, she learned that arriving Seminoles had groups of slaves among them. She went and searched for Rose – the woman given to her by the Prophet – and found her living among the Seminoles:

She picked her out of a number of negroes and Rose did not know her until she told her name, when she instantly threw her arms about her mistress, Milly, and declared that she was her old mistress. Rose has now seven children, which Milly claims, but says her husband does not belong to her.[8]

Having taken down Milly's account regarding the slaves, Hitchcock then asked her about the incident in 1818 when she had saved the life of Duncan McCrimmon. He noted that her "eyes were very animated as she gave this account" and described her as a "good looking woman now" who "must have been a beautiful girl." Milly told the colonel that she was a little girl at the time if the incident, "the size of her daughter now."[9]

The much-travelled Creek Pocahontas told Hitchcock the full story of how she had saved McCrimmon. She described hearing a war whoop as two warriors arrived at their village on the Wakulla with the young soldier as their prisoner. She discounted the stories that the followers of the Prophet were preparing to burn him at the stake, indicating instead that they planned to shoot him. She told the major that she had first gone to her father, who had explained that under law the life of the young man was in the hands of his captors. She then went to the two warriors holding him and pleaded that they spare him. One of them said that the soldier should die to bring justice to his two sisters who had been killed by white troops. "She told him that to kill a white man would not bring back his sisters," Hitchcock wrote, "and that he (i.e. McCrimmon) was but a boy and had not the "head" of a man to guide him."[10]

The bereaved warrior was not immediately convinced, but Milly continued to talk and reason with him:

...I finally persuaded him, and he said that if the young man would agree to have his head shaved, and dress like an Indian, and live among them, they would save his life.' She then proposed the conditions to the white man, which were joyfully accepted; and the Indians changed the contemplated death scene into a frolic. They shaved the young man's head, excepting the scalp lock, which was ornamented with feathers, and, after painting him and providing him an Indian dress, he was set at liberty and adopted as one of the tribe.[11]

McCrimmon's membership in the Prophet's band was short-lived, of course, and within a few days he was turned over to the Spanish at San Marcos de Apalache in exchange for a supply of rum.

Major Hitchcock was greatly moved by Milly Francis and her story. A man who by and large was sympathetic to the condition of the American Indians, he reported truthfully to Washington about the extent and severity of the frauds being perpetrated on the Creeks by unscrupulous contractors, agents, traders and outlaws.

On April 13, 1842, Colonel Hitchcock penned the following letter to J.C. Spencer, the Secretary of War, pleading that something be done to relieve the abject poverty of Milly and her family:

WASHINGTON CITY, April 13, 1842.

SIR: I have the honor to report that, in my recent visit to the Creek nation of Indians, I found a Creek woman, named Milly, a daughter of the celebrated Prophet Francis, the Creek chief who was executed by order of General Jackson in the Seminole war of 1817-'18; and, believing that the circumstances of her history presented a case of very peculiar interest, I made it a point to obtain from herself a statement of her conduct in 1818, when, as public history has already recorded, she saved the life of an American citizen who was a prisoner in the power of some of her tribe. The history states that the white man was about to be burned alive, but was saved by the interposition of the prophet's daughter. Being in the vicinity of the Indian girl, near the mouth of the Verdigris river, and being acquainted with a portion of her history, I rode several miles to hear her story from herself.

I had been informed that she has a claim to some negro property, now held by the Seminoles; and I first questioned her in relation to her claim, and then directed her mind back to 1818, and told her I had heard that she had saved the life of a white man in the war of that year. She answered that she had, and immediately gave me a minute and very graphic account of the circumstances.

139

Milly Francis

I shall not be able to do justice to her story, and can only embrace the main features of it. She began by saying that an elder sister and herself were playing on the bank of the river Appalachicola, when they heard a war-cry, which they understood to signify that a prisoner had been taken. They immediately went in the direction of the cry, and found a white man, entirely naked, tied to a tree, and two young Indian warriors, with their rifles, dancing around him, preparatory to putting him to death, as was their right, according to custom, they having taken him a prisoner. She explained to me that in such cases the life of a prisoner is in the hands of the captors – that event he chiefs have no authority in the case. Milly was then but 15 or 16 years of age. "The prisoner was a young man," said Milly, "and seemed very much frightened, and looked wildly around to see if any body would help him." "I thought it was a pity," said she, "that a young man like him should be put to death; and I spoke to my father, and told him that it was a pity to kill him – that he had no head to go to war with," (meaning that the young man must have acted upon the advice of others, and not upon his own suggestion, in going to war.) "My father told me," continued Milly, "that he could not save him, and advised me to speak to the Indians, and I did so; but one of them was very much enraged, saying he had lost two sisters in the war, and would put the prisoner to death. I told him," said Milly, "that it would not bring his sisters back to kill the young man; and so, talking to him for some time, I finally persuaded him; and he said that if the young man would agree to have his head shaved, and dress like an Indian, and live among them, they would save his life." She then proposed the conditions to the white man, which were joyfully accepted; and the Indians changed the contemplated death scene to a frolic. They shaved the young man's head, excepting the scalp lock, which was ornamented with feathers; and, after painting him, and providing him an Indian dress, he was set at liberty, and adopted as one of the tribe.

Some time afterwards, the young man proposed marriage; but Milly says she did not save his life for that, and declined his proposals.

140

I asked Milly how she now lived. She told me that she was very poor, and had to work very hard; that her father was put to death in the war, and her mother and sister were dead. Her husband was also dead. Of eight children she had but three living, two of whom were young girls, and one a boy, too young yet to help her. But she said that if she could recover her property from the Seminoles, she could live very well.

She is now about 40 years of age; and after having seen her, and being entirely satisfied of the truth of her story, I am induced to recommend that her case be laid before Congress, with an application for a small pension for her support in her old age, in consideration of her extraordinary and successful interposition, by which, in 1818, the life of an American citizen was saved from a cruel death from the hands of savages. A small pension, ($50 or $75 a year,) with a clear exposition of the grounds of its allowance, may have a salutary influence upon savage customs in future times. A more suitable occasion than the present, it is presumed, can hardly be expected. Milly has now no husband or brother, or any near connexion, to provide for her, and is in need – with a fine promising son, indeed, but too young to be of service to his mother; and, owing to pledges made to the Seminoles, it is probable she will not be able to recover possession of some negro property, now held by the Seminoles, belonging to her.

The story of Milly Francis is recorded in a volume entitled "Indian Wars," in which there is a picture representing the preparations for putting the white man to death, while the Indian girl is represented as pleading for his life to her father.

The circumstances are familiarly spoken of in the Indian country; and there is no reason to doubt the truth of the story, except that Milly told me herself that the young man would have been shot, and not burned to death, as the story represents.

I have the honor to be, very respectfully, your obedient servant,

E.A. HITCHCOCK,
Lieutenant Colonel 3d Infantry, &c.[12]

The letter from Colonel Hitchcock to Secretary Spencer is one of the most remarkable documents in American history. For the first time in all of the years of his country's dealings with the original inhabitants of the land, a United States Army officer was recommending that a woman receive a military pension even though she had belonged to the family of one of the nation's most bitter enemies.

Hitchcock made the text of his appeal available to the newspapers and the story of his request spread like wildfire across the nation. Milly Francis once again became a household name as editors across the United States updated their readers on the deplorable nature of her current condition and reminded them of the mercy she had shown to a young Georgia soldier many years before. Editors everywhere opined that something should be done to relieve her suffering.

Likewise moved by Hitchcock's plea, Secretary Spencer wrote to the Chairman of the House Committee on Indian Affairs, Representative James Cooper, recommending that Congress move on the colonel's recommendation:

War Department,
Washington, April 16, 1842.

SIR: I have the honor to transmit, herewith, a report of Lieutenant Colonel Hitchcock, in the case of Milly, an Indian woman of the Creek nation, who, in 1818, when quite young, saved the life of a white prisoner captured by her tribe and sentenced to be put to death.

She is now residing with her people at the West – a poor destitute widow, without the means of support, having lost all her property, and her children too young to provide for her or themselves. Similar to the romantic scene in our early history, her peculiar case demands our sympathy and admiration, and most strongly commends itself to the favorable consideration of your committee and of the House. I would recommend that a pension for life, of eight dollars per month, be allowed her by the Government. It may be an inducement to preserve the lives of those captured by hostile Indians, and be the means of mitigating to a great degree the barbarous cruelty of savage warfare.

I have the honor to be, with great respect, your obedient servant,

J.C. Spencer.[13]

As the public clamored that something be done to assist Milly, the House Committee of Indian Affairs deliberated the matter. On Tuesday, February 28, 1843, Representative Cooper made the following report on behalf of his committee:

> *The committee on Indian Affairs, to whom was submitted a communication from the Secretary of War, recommending that a pension be granted to Milly, an Indian woman of the Creek nation, report:*

That it appears, from the communication of the Secretary of War and the accompanying statement of Lieutenant Colonel Hitchcock, as well as from the published and accredited history of the period, that, in 1818, during the Indian war in the South, Milly, the proposed object of the bounty of the Government, saved the life of an American citizen, who had been taken prisoner by several warriors of her tribe, and who was about to be put to death by them, when he was rescued by her energetic and humane interposition. The act of this Indian girl revives the recollection of an event in our colonial annals – the rescue of Captain Smith by the daughter of Powhattan, the celebrated Pocahontas.

Milly is the daughter of the Prophet Francis, a distinguished Creek chief, who acquired a melancholy celebrity from his execution by order of General Jackson during the Indian war of 1817-'18. At the time she performed the action which is so ennobling to her character, she was under sixteen years of age, her nation was at war with the United States, and her father was one of the most decided and indefatigable enemies of the white people – circumstances all of which go to exhibit her conduct in a more excellent and exalted point of view. At the time the prisoner was brought in by his captors, Milly and an elder sister were playing on the bank of the Appalachicola river in the vicinity of the Indian camp, when they were startled, in the midst of their sports, by the peculiar war-cry which announced that a prisoner had been taken. They immediately went in the direction of the cry; and, on arriving at the place, found a young

143

white man stripped naked, bound to a tree, and his captors preparing to put him to death. On observing this, Milly instantly went to her father, who, as before stated, was the Prophet Francis, and the principal chief of the nation, and besought him to save the prisoner's life. This he declined, saying at the same time that he had no power to do so. She then turned to his captors, and begged them to spare the life of the white man; but one of them who had lost two sisters in the war refused to listen to her supplications in behalf of the prisoner, declaring that his life should atone for the wrongs which he had received at the hands of the white people. The active humanity of Milly would not be discouraged. She reasoned and entreated, telling the vindictive savage who was bent on the destruction of the prisoner that his death would not restore his sisters to life. After a long time spent in her generous effort, she succeeded in rescuing the prisoner from the dreadful death to which he had been doomed by his cruel captors. The condition on which his life was finally spared, was that he would shave his head after the Indian fashion and adopt their dress and manner of living. To this he joyfully assented.

Some time afterwards the white man sought his benefactress in marriage, but she declined, and subsequently married one of her own people. Her husband is now dead. Her father was put to death in the war of 1817-'18, and her mother and sister have since died. She is now friendless and poor, residing among her people in their new country, near the mouth of the Verdigris river. She has three children, a boy and two girls, all too young to provide for themselves, and consequently dependent upon their mother for support.

Under these circumstances, the Secretary of War recommends that a pension of eight dollars per month be allowed her during the remainder of her life. The committee see a strong argument in favor of this dispensation of the bounty of the Government, not only in the relief which it will afford the immediate recipient, whose conduct has so well deserved it, but also in the effect which it is calculated to produce by teaching the still uncivilized though gradually improving people to whom she belongs the value of humanity. This act of the Government, furnishing at once a proof of its gratitude and benevolence, will show them the estimation in which deeds of mercy are held by it, as well as the rewards which it bestows on those who perform them.

The power of the Government to confer such bounties has been frequently exercised. In 1824, Congress passed an act granting to General Lafayette and his heirs two hundred thousand dollars and a township of land. In 1834, an act was passed granting two hundred and thirty-five Polish exiles, transported to the United States by order of the Emperor of Austria, thirty-six sections of land, within the limits of the State of Illinois or the Territory of Michigan. The act by which pensions are granted to the widows of officers and soldiers of the army of the United States is an exercise of the same power founded on the same general principle. But it is enough to say that the Government which does not possess its power to pay its debts of gratitude, and to perform acts of beneficence and charity, would be unworthy of the respect and affections of its citizens.

Believing that the act of this Indian woman presents a proper case for the exercise of the gratitude and bounty of the Government, the committee report a bill allowing her a pension of ninety-six dollars per annum during her life.[14]

Ironically, the township of land given to the Marquis de Lafayette that Representative Cooper mentioned as an example of the power of the federal government to relieve Milly's suffering was in Tallahassee, Florida, within just a few miles of the places where she had saved McCrimmon's life and where she had witnessed the executions of both her father and her friend, Robert Ambrister.

Congress, even in those days, was a slow moving entity. The first bill of relief for Milly Francis died at the end of the 1843 session. Disappointed, Colonel Hitchcock once again lobbied the powers in Washington to do something to relieve the woman's suffering. On January 10, 1844, he wrote to Brigadier General Daniel Parker asking for his help:

Jefferson Barracks, Mo.,
January 10, 1844.

DEAR SIR: I hope you will excuse my asking your attention to the case of the Creek woman, Milly Francis, which you may remember was not finally acted upon in the last session of Congress. It should not be forgotten that Milly Francis is the daughter of the celebrated Creek prophet, who was sacrificed from a severe, however necessary policy, in 1818, by order of General Jackson; and that this daughter, when very young, saved the life of an American citizen, a prisoner to the Creeks in 1813; and that she is now a helpless widow with young children, and is living in the Creek nation, a few miles from Fort Gibson.

Very respectfully, your obedient servant,
E.A. HITCHCOCK,
Lieut. Col. 3d Infantry.[15]

Parker forwarded Hitchcock's letter to the House Committee on Indian Affairs, expressing his support for the requested relief. The bill authorizing a pension of $96 per year was reintroduced and this time received speedy passage in both the House and Senate. It was signed by President John Tyler on June 17, 1844.

The bill passed for the relief of Milly Francis included two provisions, both of which were unique in American history:

...[T]he Secretary of War be, and he is hereby authorized and directed to pay to Milly, an Indian woman of the Creek nation, and daughter of the prophet Francis, a pension at a rate of ninety-six dollars per annum, payable semi-annually during her natural life, as a testimonial of the gratitude and bounty of the United States, for the humanity displayed by her in the war of one thousand eight hundred and seventeen and one thousand eight hundred and eighteen in saving the life of an American citizen, who was a prisoner in the hands of her people and about to be put to death by them; the said pension to commence and take effect from the fourth day of September, one thousand eight hundred and forty-three.

Section 2. And it is further enacted, That the Secretary of War be, and he is hereby authorized and directed to procure, and transmit to the said Milly, a medal with appropriate devices impressed thereon, of the value of not exceeding twenty dollars, and an additional testimonial of the gratitude of the United States.[16]

The second section of the bill provided – for the first time in the history of the United States – for the issuance of a special medal of honor from Congress to an American woman. While she is not named as such on most modern lists, Milly Francis was the first person ever to receive a Congressional Medal of Honor.

Washington being Washington, it was not until June 1847 – three years after the passage of the desperately needed bill for Milly's relief – that the wheels of government began to turn. The Commissioner of Indian Affairs authorized the carrying out of the act and on March 16, 1848 – another year later – the Treasury Department issued a warrant for $20 to pay for the medal approved by Congress.[17]

It was not until May 1848, more than five years after she visited with Colonel Hitchcock at the little trading post on the Arkansas River, that Milly Francis learned of the relief being provided to her by the government of a grateful nation. Sadly, it was too late:

Creek Agency, June 1, 1848

Sir:

I had the honor to receive on the 7th Ulto. your communication, with enclosure, of the 7th of April last relating to the Act of Congress, granting to Milly, daughter of the Prophet Francis a pension for her generosity in saving the life of a White man. The same day I received information that she was laying dangerous ill – I immediately visited her, & found her as I was informed, in dying circumstances, and I regret to say in a most wretched condition. I immediately procured medical aid, & done all that was possible to alleviate her sufferings. – I read your letter to her, (she comprehending English perfectly) at which she was so highly elated, that I flattered myself she was recovering – but my hopes were fallacious, her disease was consumption, she died on the 19th Ulto. being about fifty years old. She died a Christian, a devout member of the Baptist Church, has left, two sons and a daughter the Youngest of the boys, is at present at Col. Johnsons Academy in Ky – She informed me, that at the time the act was rendered which saved the life of Capt. McCrimmon, she never expected any pecuniary reward, her family were rich, she did not require it. She had however become very poor - & she was very grateful for the notice taken of her by the Govt., &c. &c. –

I beg leave to ask for information as to how, I shall procure the Amt. of the Pension in arrearage - & how I am to dispose of it.

> I am Sir
> Very Respectfully,
> Your Obdt. St.
> James Logan, Creek Agent[18]

Milly Francis died in poverty at her little cabin overlooking the forks of the Arkansas, Verdigris and Neosho Rivers on May 19, 1848. She was buried there, far away from her childhood home on the Alabama River, in a grave that is lost to time. Tradition holds that one of her children rests beside her. Of the eight to whom she gave birth, only three survived to outlive their mother.

Arrangements were made by government officials for the pension monies due her at the time of her death to be held by an agent and used to provide for the needs of her children until it was expended. The medal was approved and cast and the records of the Office of Indian Affairs indicate that it was given to a Creek delegation then in Washington to be carried to the Nation and given to her oldest son. It remains a treasured artifact to her descendants, a number of whom still live in the Muskogee (Creek) Nation of Oklahoma.[19]

Indian University was established on the site of her home in 1880, just forty-two years after her death. Its name was later changed to Bacone College in honor of its founder and first professor. The school has a long tradition of service to students from the Muskogee (Creek) and Cherokee Nations and is a noteworthy part of Oklahoma's past, present and future. In 1933, the faculty and students of the college erected a monument near the center of their campus to pay tribute to the memory of Milly Francis.[20]

The monument is still there today, the words inscribed on the massive rock reminding all who pass of the story of the Creek Pocahontas and the proximity of her grave. Its location on the grounds of a college that has done so much good for students from the Muskogee (Creek) Nation is a fitting place. Milly Francis, through her act of mercy and charity sixty-two years before the founding of the college, caused a ripple in the conscience of a nation that we continue to feel today.

---

[1] Muster Roll of deceased officers and soldiers of the Mounted Regiment of Creek Indian Volunteers," prepared by Major W.G. Freeman, September 28, 1837, Senate Executive Document 55, 30th Congress, 1st Session, 1848.

[2] Ethan Allen Hitchcock, *Fifty Years in Camp and Field*, p. 143.

[3] Ethan Allen Hitchcock, *A Traveler in Indian Territory: The Journal of Ethan Allen Hitchcock*, pp. 94-95.

[4] *Ibid.*, pp. 95-96.

[5] *Ibid.*, P. 98.

[6] *Ibid.*, P. 102.

[7] *Ibid.*, p. 103.

[8] *Ibid.*, p. 103.

[9] *Ibid.*, pp. 103-104.

[10] *Ibid.*, p. 104.

[11] Ethan Allen Hitchcock, *Fifty Years in Camp and Field*, p. 152.

[12] Ethan Allen Hitchcock to J.C. Spencer, April 16, 1842, included in House Report 274, Serial Set Volume No. 428, February 28, 1843, 27th Congress, 3rd Session.

[13] J.C. Spencer to Rep. James Cooper, April 16, 1842, included in House Report 274, Serial Set Volume No. 428, February 28, 1843, 27th Congress, 3rd Session.

[14] Report of the Committee on Indian Affairs, House Report 274, Serial Set Volume No. 428, February 28, 1843, 37th Congress, 3rd Session.

[15] Ethan Allen Hitchcock to Daniel Parker, January 10, 1844, House Report 149, Serial Set Volume No. 445, February 15, 1844, 28th Congress, 1st Session.

[16] United States Statutes at Large, Private Laws, Volume 6, pp. 928-929.

[17] Treasury Department Warrant, March 16, 1848, Office of Indian Affairs, Creek File T-86,

[18] James Logan to W. Medill, June 1, 1848, Office of Indian Affairs, Letter Book No. 41.

[19] W. Medill to Samuel M. Rutherford, July 17, 1848, Office of Indian Affairs, Letter Book No. 41.

[20] Works Progress Administration, Federal Writers Project, *Oklahoma: A Guide to the Sooner State*, pp. 337-338.

Chattahoochee Landing, along the route of Milly's return to the Creek Nation.

Fort Gaines, Milly's family was supplied here on the return to the Nation.

151

Trail of Tears crossing near Sallisaw, Oklahoma.

Fort Gibson Historic Site in Oklahoma, where the Trail of Tears ended for Milly Francis.

Photographs

Cherokee cabin in Sallisaw, Oklahoma, probably similar to Milly's home.

Wahoo Swamp Battlefield, where Milly's husband fought the Seminoles.

Battle Branch at Wahoo Swamp, where Major David Moniac was killed.

Milly Francis Monument at Bacone College in Muskogee, Oklahoma

Milly Francis is thought to be the woman on Florida's Great Seal.

The Great Seal with Milly Francis appears at the center of Florida's state flag
Both courtesy of Florida State Archives, *Florida Memory Collection.*

Conclusion

THE STORY OF MILLY FRANCIS is as much a story of America as it is the tale of a person. During her brief 45 years of life she suffered innumerable and immeasurable tragedies, but never lost her self-respect and dignity. She never raised a weapon in war, yet her life was heroic. It is appropriate that she received the nation's first Congressional Medal of Honor and she should be better remembered by present and future generations.

Milly Francis, more than any other single person in American history, began our nation's dialog with itself over the humanity and treatment of the American Indians. Her act of mercy in saving the life of Duncan McCrimmon caused the editors of our country's largest newspapers to ponder the concept that in the breast of an assumed "savage" beat a human heart. From editorial pages north and south, the discussion spread and would continue to spread, even as the United States continued its wars with the Seminole, Cheyenne, Comanche, Sioux, Apache and other nations that stood in the way of its ever-expanding frontiers. By the time of Wounded Knee, the collective conscience of the nation understood the tragedy that had been inflicted on fellow human beings simply because they wished to live their lives in their own ways.

In 1899, as part of the same pamphlet that demanded women be admitted to the University of Georgia, the Education Committee of the Georgia Federation of Women's Clubs urged that the stories of Milly Francis and Revolutionary War firebrand Nancy Hart be made required reading for all young people in the state:

> ...*Milly Francis, our Georgia Pocahontas, was quite as worthy to be canonized as the Virginia heroine. Molly Pitcher and Mrs. Dustin are but pale shades compared to Nancy Hart, "the War Woman," that sharp-tongued Georgia Cracker, that "honey of a patriot."*[1]

The exact site of Milly's grave has been forgotten, but is thought to be in the vicinity of Bacone College. There is a small cemetery at the school in which can be found headstones and monuments marking the graves of its founder, professors, students and others who died while serving there. Several unmarked graves can be seen in the little burial ground. Perhaps one of these is her final resting place.

In addition to the monument that stands in her honor at Bacone College, several other locations now pay tribute to Milly Francis. Nearby Fort Gibson State Historic Site, for example, includes a reconstructed stockade and later buildings from the fort that served as the end of the Trail of Tears for the Creek Nation. Exhibits and restored rooms explain the long history of the fort.

The Trail of Tears National Historic Trail touches several sites associated with Milly Francis. Fort Smith National Historic Site in Fort Smith is near the site where the steamboat grounded while carrying her west in 1836. The park features a Trail of Tears Overlook at the confluence of the Arkansas and Poteau Rivers that tells the story of the different American Indian nations included in the forced migration. Near Lewisburg, Potts Inn is now a museum. The current structure was built in 1850, but stands at the site where Tuckabatchee Hadjo's group camped in the cold winter of 1836.

A small monument honors Milly as "Princess Malee" on the grounds of San Marcos de Apalache Historic State Park in St. Marks, Florida. It stands near – possibly even on – the site where her father was hanged by order of General Jackson in 1818. He is buried somewhere nearby in an unmarked grave. The ruins of the old Spanish fort, a place once familiar to her, can still be seen. Inside these stone ramparts, the daughters of the Spanish commandant helped fit the dresses that the Prophet Francis had brought home from England as gifts for his daughter and helped console her after the shooting of Robert Ambrister.

At Fort Gadsden Historic Site in Florida's Apalachicola National Forest, a historical marker tells the story of Milly Francis and notes that it was from the fort that Duncan McCrimmon disappeared in 1818. The earthworks of the fort that was being built at the time he went on his unfortunate fishing trip are well preserved and can still be seen, as can the traces of the "Negro Fort" blown up by American forces in 1816. Milly Francis lived here for a time in 1814-1815 and it was from Fort Gadsden that she and her family made their way home to the Creek Nation in 1818. It was also within its walls of earth and log that she declined the proposal of Duncan McCrimmon.

Other sites associated with Milly Francis are commemorated in various ways. Holy Ground Battlefield Park stands near the site of the town on the Alabama River where Milly lived as a young girl and witnessed her father's efforts to convert the Creek people to his new religion. The actual site of Holy Ground is across the creek to the west of today's park, but its boardwalk provides a beautiful view of the Alabama River and interpretive panels tell the story of the Battle of

Conclusion

Holy Ground. The park is between Montgomery and Selma in White Hall, Alabama.

In Pensacola, to which the Prophet Francis fled with his family following the collapse of the Red Stick movement in Alabama, the Historic Pensacola Village preserves a number of historic homes and structures, some of which were standing in 1818. A monument to Andrew Jackson stands nearby on the Plaza Ferdinand, commemorating his acceptance of the transfer of Florida from Spain to the United States in 1821. Within Gulf Islands National Seashore, visitors to Fort Barrancas can still walk the ramparts of the Bateria de San Antonio, part of the fort evacuated by the British at the time of Jackson's attack on Pensacola in 1814. Colonel Nicolls and Captain Woodbine once walked these walls, as too did the Prophet Josiah Francis and Peter McQueen.

On the Great Seal of Florida, seen at the state capital in Tallahassee and on the State Flag of Florida, can be seen the image of an American Indian woman. She sprinkles flowers on the ground in symbolic tribute to the beautiful place named the "Land of Flowers" by the Spanish. Legend holds that the figure is a representation of Milly Francis.

In nearby Wakulla County, one of the most magnificent springs on the face of the earth rises from the ground to form the Wakulla River. Milly Francis and her sister once played by its crystal clear waters and just a few miles downstream from today's Edward Ball Wakulla Springs State Park is the spot where she saved the life of Duncan McCrimmon. The site is now in the Hyde Park subdivision. Guides at Wakulla Springs have long told visitors that the name is a Seminole Indian word that means "strange and mysterious waters." Although modern scholars disagree on this interpretation, it somehow seems appropriate. After all, the horror movie *Creature from the Black Lagoon* was filmed on the Wakulla. Boat cruises are available at the dock in the state park to carry visitors down the Wakulla into a region of cypress trees, birds and alligators that is little changed from the days of the Seminole Wars. Some say the spirits of the ancient Indians can still be seen there on stormy nights and foggy mornings. Perhaps the family of Milly Francis is among them.

---

[1] *New York Tribune*, May 15, 1899, p. 7.

References

Articles

Cox, Dale, "The Battle of Fort Bowyer," copyrighted online article at website www.exploresouthernhistory.com, 2012.

Davis, T. Frederick, "Milly Francis and Duncan McKrimmon: an Authentic Florida Pocahontas", *The Florida Historical Quarterly*, Volume 21, No. 3, January 1943.

Sugden, John, "The Southern Indians in the War of 1812: The Closing Phase," *The Florida Historical Quarterly*, Volume LX, Number 3, January 1982.

Books

Banks, John, *Diary of John Banks*, n.d.

Codrington, Edward, *Memoir of the life of Admiral Sir Edward Codrington*, Volume II, London, 1875.

Cox, Dale, *The Scott Massacre of 1817: A Seminole War Battle in Gadsden County, Florida*, West Gadsden Historical Society, 2013.

Crockett, David, *A Narrative of the Life of David Crockett, of the State of Tennessee*, Philadelphia and Baltimore, 1834.

Eaton, John Henry, John Reid, *The Life of Major General Jackson*,

Edmunds, David R., *The Shawnee Prophet*, University of Nebraska Press, 1985.

Hitchcock, Ethan Allen, *Fifty Years in Camp and Field*, (W.A. Croffut, editor), Knickerbocker Press, New York, 1909.

Hitchcock, Ethan Allen, *Traveler in Indian Territory: The Journal of Ethan Allen Hitchcock*, (Grant Foreman, editor), Torch Press, Cedar Rapids, 1930.

Parton, James, *Life of Andrew Jackson*, Volume 2, Houghton, Mifflen and Company, 1888.

Whittemore, Henry, *The Heroes of the American Revolution and their Descendants*, The Heroes of the Revolution Publishing Co., 1897,

Maps

Pintado, Josef, Map of the Apalachicola River, ca. 1815, Library of Congress.

Newspapers

Alexandria Gazette, May 21, 1814.
Alexandria Herald, July 4, 1811.
Camden Gazette, January 7, 1819
Charleston Courier, December 17, 1811.
Daily National Intelligencer, September 13, 1813.
Federal Republican, December 20, 1811.
Georgia Journal, December 22, 1818.
Milledgeville Reflector, October 13, 1818; November 2, 1818.
New York Tribune, May 15, 1899.
Ohio Republican, February 12, 1814.
Poulson's American Daily Advertiser, December 23, 1811.
Raleigh Minerva, 1813.
Rhode-Island American, December 31, 1811.
Richmond Enquirer, September 7, 1813.
Savannah Republican, December 17, 1811.
Trenton Federalist, December 21, 1818.
Universal Gazette, September 9, 1813.

Official Correspondence and Reports

Arbuckle, Matthew, to David B. Mitchell, Agent of the Creek Nation, August 31, 1818, Office of the Adjutant General, Letters Received, 1805-1821, National Archives.

Letter from Fort Gadsden (probably written by Lt. Col. Matthew Arbuckle), August 31, 1818, published in the Milledgeville Reflector, October 13, 1818, p. 3.

Big Warrior, Alexander Cornells and William McIntosh to Benjamin Hawkins, April 26, 1813, *American State Papers, Indian Affairs*, Volume 1.

Butler, Robert, Brig. Gen. Daniel Parker, Adjutant and Inspector General, May 3, 1818, *American State Papers, Military Affairs*, Volume 1, p. 703.

Chiefs, Indian Agreement, WO/1/143/147-150.

Cornells, Alexander, to Benjamin Hawkins, June 22, 1813, *American State Papers, Indian Affairs*, Volume 1.

Claiborne, Ferdinand L., Claiborne to Gov. Willie Blount, January 1, 1814, published in the *Ohio Republican*, Volume I, Issue 38, p. 2 February 12, 1814.

Eneah Micco, and other chiefs to the Secretary of War, April 8, 1831, Office of Indian Affairs, "Creek Emigration," Document II, p. 424.

Francis, Josiah, i.e. "Joshua" Francis, Yaholloasaptko, Hopoyhisilyholla to British Commander at St. George's Island, June 9, 1814, CP, 2328, pp. 28-29.

Freeman, W.G., Muster Roll of deceased officers and soldiers of the Mounted Regiment of Creek Indian Volunteers," September 28, 1837, Senate Executive Document 44, 30th Congress, 1st Session, 1848.

Hawkins, Benjamin, to Big Warrior, Little Prince and other Chiefs, June 16, 1814, *American State Papers, Indian Affairs*, Volume 1.

Hawkins, Benjamin, Description of the Battle of New Orleans by an anonymous Red Stick chief as written in Hawkins to Gov. Peter Early, February 12, 1815, Telamon Cuyler Collection, UGA, Box 76, Folder 25, Document 20.

Hawkins, Benjamin, to Peter Early, February 26, 1815, Telamon Cuyler Collection, UGA, Box 76, Folder 25, Document 23.

Henry, Robert, Admiral Alexander Cochrane, November 22, 1814, CP, 2328, p. 126.

Hitchcock, Ethan Allen, to J.C. Spencer, April 16, 1842, included in House Report 274, Serial Set Volume No. 428, February 28, 1843, 27th Congress, 3rd Session.

Hitchcock, Ethan Allen, to Daniel Parker, January 10, 1844, House Report 149, Serial Set Volume No. 445, February 15, 1844, 28th Congress, 1st Session.

Jackson, Andrew, to John C. Calhoun, Secretary of War, March 25, 1818, *American State Papers, Military Affairs*, Volume 1, pp. 698-699.

Jackson, Andrew, to Capt. Isaac McKeever, March 26, 1818, from James Parton, *Life of Andrew Jackson*, Volume 2, pp. 447-448.

Jackson, Andrew, , General Orders of April 26, 1818, issued by Robert Butler, Adjutant General, *British and Foreign State Papers*, Volumes 6-7, p. 792.

Jackson, Andrew, The Memorial of Andrew Jackson, Major General in the Army of The United States, and Commander of the Southern Division," March 6, 1820, British and Foreign State Papers, Volumes 6-7, pp. 758-777.

Luengo, Francisco, to Gov. Don Jose Masot, May 14, 1818, *American State Papers, Military Affairs*, Volume 1, p. 711.

Logan, James, to W. Medill, June 1, 1848, Office of Indian Affairs, Letter Book No. 41.

Kasitah Chiefs to to Lt. J.T. Sprague, December 21, 1836, enclosed in Sprague to Harris, April 1, 1837, OIL, "Creek Emigration" file.

Medill, W., to Samuel M. Rutherford, July 17, 1848, Office of Indian Affairs, Letter Book No. 41.

Moniac, Samuel, "The Deposition of Samuel Manac," August 2, 1813, SPR 26, Alaama Department of Archives and History.

Mushulatuba to George S. Gaines, July 15, 1813, published in the *Richmond Enquirer*, September 7, 1813.

Pearson, J.G. to Joseph Graham, June 1, 1814 (published in the *Raleigh Minerva*).

Nicolls, Edward, to Adm. Alexander Cochrane, August 12, 1814, CP, 2328, pp. 59-62.

Rodgers, Dr. J.B., Eyewitness Account of the First Seminole War as quoted by James Parton, *Life of Andrew Jackson*, Volume 2, Houghton, Mifflen and Company, 1888.

Sprague, J.T., Journal of Lt. J.T. Sprague, included in Sprague to Harris, April 1, 1837, OIA, "Creek Emigration" file.

Spencer, J.C., to Rep. James Cooper, April 16, 1842, included in House Report 274, Serial Set Volume No. 428, February 28, 1843, 27th Congress, 3rd Session.

Talosee Fixico, runner from Tuckabatchee, to Benjamin Hawkins, July 5, 1813, *American State Papers, Indian Affairs*, Volume 1.

U.S. Government, Creek Nation Census of 1832, Certified May 1 and May 13, 1833, Senate Document 512, 23rd Congress, 1st Session.

U.S. Government, Report of the Committee on Indian Affairs, House Report 274, Serial Set Volume No. 428, February 28, 1843, 37th Congress, 3rd Session.

U.S. Government, Treasury Department Warrant, March 16, 1848, Office of Indian Affairs, Creek File T-86.

U.S. Government, Works Progress Administration, Federal Writers Project, *Oklahoma: A Guide to the Sooner State*

Private Correspondence and Documents

Anonymous Gentleman in the Executive Department Milledgeville, GA to a resident of Alexandria, VA, published in the *Alexandria Gazette*, Volume XIV, Issue 4165, May 21, 1814.

Arbuckle, Matthew, Letter from Fort Gadsden (probably written by Lt. Col. Matthew Arbuckle), August 31, 1818, published in the *Milledgeville Reflector*, October 13, 1818, p. 3.

Arbuckle, Matthew, to the Editor, December 1, 1818, published in the *Georgia Journal*, December 22, 1818, p. 3.

References

Doyle, Edward, John Innerarity, July 11, 1817, *Florida Historical Quarterly*, Volume 18, Issue 02, October 1939, p. 136.

Hitchcock, Ethan Allen, Journal of Ethan Allen Hitchcock, National Archives.

Toulmin, Harry, Letter of July 29, 1813, published in the *Universal Gazette*, Volume XI, Issue 819, September 9, 1813.

Toulmin, Harry, A Respectable Gentleman to Col. Benjamin Hawkins, August 13, 1813, published in the *Daily National Intelligencer*, Volume I, Issue 218, September 13, 1813.

Samuel M. Rutherford, July 17, 1848, Office of Indian Affairs, Letter Book No. 41.

About the Author

Dale Cox is a Southern writer and historian with more than fourteen books to his credit. His critically-acclaimed book, *The Battle of Marianna, Florida*, was named best in its category by Civil War Books & Authors. *The Battle of Natural Bridge, Florida*, Cox's history of the 1865 Confederate defense of Tallahassee, was hailed by reviewers as the "excellent." *The Scott Massacre of 1817: A Seminole War Battle in Gadsden County, Florida* overlaps in many ways the story of Milly Francis. Published to support the preservation and interpretation efforts of the West Gadsden Historical Society, the book is among the author's personal favorites and provides the first in depth history of the beginning days of Florida's Seminole Wars.

Another of Cox's books, *The Claude Neal Lynching: The 1934 Murders of Claude Neal and Lola Cannady*, has drawn widespread attention and acclaim. The most detailed account of the infamous 1934 incident to date, the book is used as a key reference by classes at Florida State University.

His other books include *Two Egg, Florida*; *A Christmas in Two Egg, Florida*; *The Battle of Massard Prairie: The 1864 Confederate Attacks on Fort Smith, Arkansas,* and *Old Parramore: The History of a Florida Ghost Town*. He also has written multiple volumes on the histories of Jackson and Gadsden Counties in Florida. *A Christmas in Two Egg, Florida* has been adapted for the stage and is performed annually during the holiday season.

Cox has appeared on numerous television programs and is a popular guest speaker. A lifetime member of the West Gadsden Historical Society, he also is a member of the Friends of Bellamy Bridge, the Friends of Florida Caverns State Park, the Walton County Heritage Association, the Luke Lott Camp of the Sons of Confederate Veterans and numerous other heritage-based organizations.

He is publisher of www.exploresouthernhistory.com, a travel website that serves the growing heritage and eco-tourism communities. The site serves more than 275,000 unique users and is viewed millions of times.

A descendent of the Yuchi leaders Efa Hadjo and Efa Emathla, he has lived his life deeply immersed in the rich heritage of the Creek Indians. Cox was the 2012 Citizen of the Year for Jackson County, Florida, and has been inducted into the Bonnie Blue Society of the Sons of Confederate Veterans, an organization for authors of note. He has been awarded the Jefferson Davis Medal by the United Daughters of the Confederacy and has been honored for his historic preservation efforts by numerous other organizations, including the Children of the American Revolution, the Daughters of the American Revolution and the Order of the Confederate Rose.

A Christian, Dale Cox is the father of two grown sons, William and Alan. He resides near the unique little community of Two Egg, Florida, with his constant canine companion, Goober D. Dogg.

Other books by Dale Cox include:

The Battle of Marianna, Florida
The Battle of Natural Bridge, Florida: The Confederate Defense of Tallahassee
The Battle of Massard Prairie: The 1864 Confederate Attacks on Fort Smith, Arkansas
The Claude Neal Lynching: The 1934 Murders of Claude Neal and Lola Cannady
The Early History of Gadsden County
The Ghost of Bellamy Bridge: 10 Stories of Ghosts & Monsters from Jackson County, Florida
The History of Jackson County, Florida (Volumes 1 & 2)
The Scott Massacre of 1817: A Seminole War Battle in Gadsden County, Florida
Old Parramore: The History of a Florida Ghost Town
Two Egg, Florida: A Collection of Ghost Stories, Legends & Unusual Facts
A Christmas in Two Egg, Florida

His books are available at www.exploresouthernhistory.com.

Index

Made in the USA
Charleston, SC
30 December 2013